Mathematical modeling in life sciences: an introduction

Michael Yampolsky

...the weather model predicted torrential rain...

Grant me the serenity to accept that some natural phenomena are too messy and unpredictable to be modeled, courage to propose simple mathematical models for the phenomena into which insight could be gained, and wisdom to know the difference.

Based on the *Serenity Prayer* by R. Niebuhr

Contents

Preface

My original motivation for writing these notes was not very original. I suggested a course on the subject for third year science majors – it seemed like a good idea at the time. There were several good textbooks already in existence, covering more or less the same "standard" material – each of them quite possibly better than this one, but none of them quite matching my taste. I taught the course using one of them, and started developing my own supplementary material. Natural laziness would probably stop me from going any further, but a year later, in the Fall of 2020, I had to teach the same course during the time of the coronavirus pandemic. Now the lectures had to be delivered online, which made having extensive prepared notes much more important to the students. The events of the pandemic also brought into focus the modern importance of mathematical modeling. Fascinating arguments over epidemic models – with major real-life consequences – would play out in the media and on the internet in real time. I was also stuck at home, with a lot more free time on my hands. In short, it seemed like an opportune moment for me to try writing a book like this, and so I did.

The book should be accessible to undergraduate students armed with Calculus in one and several variables and basic Linear Algebra. In other words, typical science majors in their third or fourth year. Students with a more extensive Math preparation should (hopefully) not find it boring either, but will be able to skip some of the theoretical background.

Let me conclude by expressing my gratitude to Yulia Bibilo, who was my TA for the course, and helped me greatly with developing the exercises for these notes. I am grateful to Cristobal Rojas for some very helpful criticisms. Last, but not least, I would like to thank the students who gave me their feedback as the work on this text progressed.

User guide

A set of suggested practice exercises is given at the end of each chapter. Complete solutions to most of them are given at the end of the book. Try not to peek at them and do the problems on your own first.

Harder problems are marked with ⊗ You will need to think outside of the box to do those.

The material that can be skipped on the first reading is typeset in a smaller font, like so.

A "diver" sign before a smaller font indicates a deeper dive into the subject. You may find this stuff either (a) boring or (b) fascinating – I am hoping for the latter, of course.

Here and there I have added examples of using *Maple*, a computer algebra system, for modeling. They are also typeset in a smaller font, and are preceded by a computer sign.

Framed statements are key to understanding the material, never skip those.

Mathematical models: handle with care

A good mathematical model is a toy replica of reality. It should be a good enough replica to capture the essential features of the natural phenomenon we would like to study. In this way it can give us a new intuition in our dealings with Nature. Like a children's toy, a model does not need to be too detailed, in fact, excessive details sometimes serve to obscure the truly essential features of the phenomenon we would like to study.

In Figure 1 you can see two toy airplanes. The one on the left is a die-cast detailed scaled replica of an airliner complete with the historically correct color scheme. The right-hand one is a simple folded paper airplane. Which one of the two would be a *better* model? The answer should be obvious: despite all of its fancy details, the first one misses the one most essential feature which every airplane must possess: it does not fly. The one on the right is simple, and yet all of the aerodynamic forces governing flight can be studied from it. It is by far the better model.

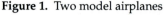

Figure 1. Two model airplanes

Simplicity is, in fact, a key feature of a good mathematical model. It is well-known to practitioners of data analysis, that a model with sufficiently many parameters can be made to fit literally anything. Is that a good thing? You be the judge. Suppose that you have discovered an interesting new type of a lizard, and you would like to study how its overall body length y relates to the length of its tail x. To determine this, you have captured five lizards, and got the following set of measurements (in inches):

tail length x	body length y
1.01	2
1.1	2.01
1.5	3.15
1.6	3.19
3	6.02

Would you care to guess what the relation between x and y is? That's right, y is roughly, although not exactly, twice x.

However, the expression $2x$ does not quite match the value of y. In an attempt to improve the predictions of the model, we can first try to use a more complicated formula relating x to y. To match the data we have, it is sufficient to use a polynomial $p(x)$ of degree 4. As a general fact, for a set of $n + 1$ points $(x_0, y_0), (x_1, y_1), \ldots, (x_n, y_n)$ there exists a unique polynomial of degree n

$$p(x) = a_n x^n + a_{n-1} x^{n-1} + \cdots + a_1 x + a_0$$

whose graph passes through these points, that is, $p(x_j) = y_j$, for $0 \le j \le n$. So, at the expense of introducing $n + 1$ parameters $a_0, \ldots, a_n$, you can match a polynomial model to any set of $n + 1$ measurements of tail/body lengths of lizards *exactly*.

Figure 2. Two models for the dependence between x and y: the straight line $y = 2x$ (blue) and the polynomial $p(x)$ (red). Data points (x, y) are marked by squares.

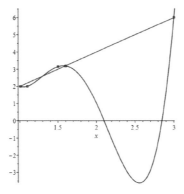

In our case,

$$y = p(x) \approx 10.51598x^4 - 72.56718x^3 + 175.47814x^2 - 177.17659x + 65.76618$$

gives an exact match to the above table.

You can look at Figure 2 to see the graphs of $p(x)$ and the line $y = 2x$. It is clear that the polynomial $p(x)$ does not describe anything remotely realistic. In particular, the "model" $p(x)$ predicts that a lizard with tail length 2.5 inches has a negative body length.

Figure 3. A lizard

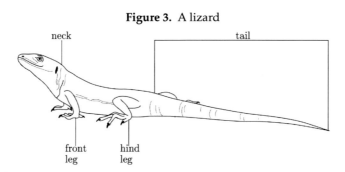

Perhaps, the measurement of the tail length alone is not sufficient to capture the total body length? What if we have added more measurements? In the table below, we see several other measurements for the same five lizards, all clearly related to the body length in some way:

tail length x	weight (in grams) w	length of hind legs h	length of front legs f	neck circumference c	body length y
1.01	0.9	0.6	0.31	1.2	2
1.1	1.3	0.5	0.27	0.95	2.01
1.5	2	1	0.6	1.4	3.15
1.6	2.2	1.3	0.6	1.4	3.19
3	6.1	2.2	1.2	3	6.02

Can we do better now, armed with this extra data? We can look for a linear relationship between y and *all* of the other parameters:

$$y = Ax + Bw + Ch + Df + Ec.$$

We can find the coefficients A, B, C, D, E to match the extended set of measurements exactly as well – by solving a linear system of five equations with five unknowns. The answer is

$$y \approx 1.4815x - 0.1127w - 0.2853h + 2.2356f + 0.0693c.$$

Before we start congratulating ourselves on developing a linear five-parameter model which agrees with the data, let us look more closely at what the formula actually says. For instance, since the coefficient of w is negative, it seems to suggest that if a lizard bulks up after a few good meals, then its overall length gets... shorter? And the largest input comes from the front legs – the longer they are, the longer the body of the lizard, which makes sense. Yet for the hind legs, this relation is reversed... Our "improved" multi-parameter model does not seem to make much sense.

We could try to make things even more complicated by combining the two approaches – that is pretty much guaranteed to make things worse. By giving ourselves too much freedom to fit the data, we missed the fairly obvious relationship between x and y. The starting point of our reasoning should have been instead something like the following: *the body length should naturally increase as a function of the tail length. In the simplest scenario, one would be proportional to the other, so let us try to find m so that*

$$y = mx.$$

This simple reasoning would have immediately led us to the relation

$$y \approx 2x.$$

Indeed, this formula does not quite match the data. Maybe there are some small "hidden" terms that we should have added. Or maybe there are indeed some other measurements which would help. Or perhaps the data are just "noisy" (which is to be expected of real world data) and there are random fluctuations or errors of measurement which make it a bit off. Or all of the above. But without some new conceptual insights, the chances of improving the model by "embellishing" it with more parameters are nil. As anyone who has ever embellished a simple story by adding new details to make it sound "better" soon discovers, these details can be inconsistent and make the whole story less believable.

The inherent simplicity of successful mathematical models allows us to replace the messy, complex, and uncertain reality of the world with a simple to understand toy replica. It is easy to fall into the trap of thinking that the replica *is* the reality, and to forget about the limitations and compromises made when designing the model. For example, in 1798, Thomas Malthus famously predicted an explosion in the size of the human population which would inevitably lead to catastrophic consequences given the finite resources available to sustain life. His thinking was predicated on a simple, and seemingly correct principle: *population grows by the same proportion each year*. Indeed, this is roughly true if a limited number of years is taken into account, and translates into an exponential growth law for the population size. However, the reality is much more complex, and, in fact, population growth rate has been falling steadily for the last 40 years or so, and has turned negative in many prosperous countries. Malthusian growth model thus is useful for highlighting a problem with constraints that limited resources put on the population size, but it is not a useful tool for making long-term predictions.

In creating a mathematical description for the real world, we have to navigate between Scylla of over-complicated models having so many parameters that they would fit literally everything (and thus explain nothing) and Charybdis of letting a simplistic toy model replace the messy and complex empirical reality in our thinking. Keeping this warning in mind, let us set sail.

First steps in modeling

1.1. Fibonacci rabbits

Our first example is perhaps the most famous population growth model of all time. It was introduced by a medieval italian mathematician Leonardo of Pisa, also known as Fibonacci. In the year 1202 (!) in his book **Liber Abaci**, Fibonacci considered the growth of a population of rabbits. His idealized rabbits procreated according to the following rules:

(1) to begin with, a newly born breeding pair of rabbits is put in the field;

(2) each breeding pair reaches maturity at the age of one month;

(3) each mature breeding pair of rabbits mates once a month;

(4) one month after mating, the breeding pair produces a new breeding pair of rabbits.

Let us see how rabbit population would grow according to Fibonacci's rules. Instead of counting the total number of rabbits, we will count the breeding pairs, so let us denote by x_n the number of breeding pairs of rabbits after n months have passed. At the start, we only have one newborn pair, and thus $x_0 = 1$. After 1 month has passed, the initial pair matures, and mates – but there is still only one pair, so $x_1 = 1$. In another month, the female of the initial pair gives birth to a new breeding pair. So $x_2 = 2$. Note that of these two pairs, only one (the original pair) is mature and can mate. In accordance with rule (3), mate it will. After 3 months, two things happen: the original pair gives another birth, and the second pair matures. So $x_3 = 3$, of which two pairs are mature (and mate) and the third one is newborn.

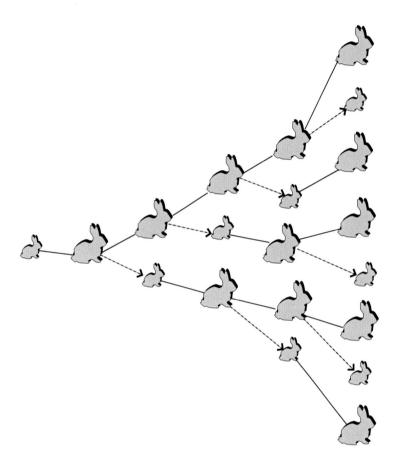

Figure 4. The growth of the Fibonacci rabbit population over the first five months. Full size pairs are mature, smaller-size pairs are newborn babies. Solid lines show the timelines of each pair, dotted arrows are new births.

You should observe the following pattern: after n months, the number of **mature** pairs is exactly the number of pairs which were already alive during the previous month (which is x_{n-1}), the rest are the newborn baby rabbits who need an extra month to mature. So of x_n pairs only x_{n-1} will procreate. This means that as the $(n+1)$-st month arrives, there will be x_{n-1}

newborns (and, of course, all of the x_n rabbits from the previous month survive).

We have thus arrived at the same rule as Fibonacci famously obtained:

(1.1.1) $$x_{n+1} = x_n + x_{n-1}.$$

Applying it, we obtain the famous Fibonacci sequence:

$$1, 1, 2, 3, 5, 8, 13, 21, \dots$$

in which, starting from the third position, each number is obtained by summing the previous two. Fibonacci's original goal was to figure out the size of the population after one year has passed. That is not difficult, of course, we just need to keep adding to see what number is in the 13th position (not 12th, since we started with x_0). But, remarkably, there is actually a formula for x_n – and we will get to it below.

1.2. Discrete time versus continuous time modeling

Fibonacci equation (1.1.1) is an example of a *discrete time model*: in it, we advance the time in discrete increments (months), and describe the size of the population at the end of each increment. We thus end up with a **sequence** of numbers x_n. In contrast, a **continuous time model** describes a function $x(t)$, which gives the size of x at any moment of time t, and not just for a specific sequence of times.

An example, familiar from Calculus, comes from radioactive decay. Its theory is based on the following simple principle: *each radioactive nucleus has the same probability of decaying over a unit of time.* So, for instance, if we measure the time t in years, then each nucleus has a chance of decaying which is equal to some constant $\lambda \in (0, 1)$ over the course of one year[1]. Alternatively, a nucleus survives a year with probability $1 - \lambda$. Generally, λ is very small. For uranium 238, which is the more common isotope found in nature, it is measured to be approximately 1.54×10^{-10}. It is tempting to think of radiactive decay as a "death" of a nucleus, but the analogy may be misleading: the theory postulates that all nuclei have the same probability

---

[1]To be precise, we should measure time in astronomical (or Julian) years, each of which consists of precisely 31,557,600 seconds, as the length of a calendar year is variable.

of decaying, independently of their age. The theory is in an excellent agreement with experiments, although it is clearly a simplification of the underlying reality, and some deviations from it have been described in physics literature at, for instance, extremely long or extremely short time scales. In other words, it is a very successful model of radioactive decay. Let us see how it can be expressed mathematically.

We start with an initial quantity P_0 (which we can calculate either in units of weight or as a total number of nuclei) of radioactive material, consisting of *a lot* of nuclei[2] – each of which survives a whole year with probability $(1 - \lambda)$. However, the decay can happen at any moment of time during the year, which will complicate the computation, as we do not know when exactly each decaying nucleus splits. Let us simplify things dramatically by assuming that all nuclei are given the chance to decay only once in a calendar year – let's say when the clock hits midnight on December 31st in Toronto. This makes the computation easy: each of the nuclei forming the initial quantity P_0 at the start of the year will decay at the year's end with probability λ; since there are a lot of them to begin with, we can simply assume that the quantity λP_0 of the material will decay, and the rest will remain. This gives us the formula

$$P_1 = (1 - \lambda)P_0$$

for the material left after one year, or

$$P_{t+1} = (1 - \lambda)P_t$$

from one year to the next. This is a discrete time model in the sense that we only allow the decay to happen at one-year time increments, not continuously.

Of course, the assumption that nuclei may only decay once a year is not a realistic one. Let us make it more realistic by partitioning a year into k equal intervals of time, and give a nucleus an opportunity to split at the end of each of these intervals. The probability of decay in a $\frac{1}{k}$-time interval is $\frac{\lambda}{k}$, and we will get

$$P_{t+\frac{1}{k}} = P_t \left(1 - \frac{\lambda}{k}\right),$$

---

[2]Recall, that one mole of uranium 238 weighs 238 grams. One mole is approximately 6.022×10^{23} particles, so there are around 2.53×10^{21} nuclei in a gram of uranium – which is, indeed, *a lot*.

which leads us to the equation

$$(1.2.1) \qquad P_{t+1} = P_t \left(1 - \frac{\lambda}{k}\right)^k$$

for the decay over a single year.

Now, to get rid of our unrealistic assumption, we should allow the nuclei to decay at **any** moment of time t. As a way of doing this, we can let k increase (or, equivalently, the time interval $\frac{1}{k}$ to shrink). If we write $P(t)$ instead of P_t, and calculate the change in $P(t)$ after a single $\frac{1}{k}$-year time increment has elapsed, we get:

$$(1.2.2) \qquad P\left(t + \frac{1}{k}\right) - P(t) = -P(t)\frac{\lambda}{k},$$

as $\frac{\lambda}{k}$-th fraction of the material will decay. Now, let us do the usual calculusy thing and divide both sides by the time increment $\frac{1}{k}$:

$$\frac{P(t + \frac{1}{k}) - P(t)}{1/k} = -\lambda P(t).$$

We can now let $k \to \infty$, so the time increments $1/k \to 0$ (and thus nuclei may split whenever they please), and the left-hand side of the equation takes the familiar form $P'(t)$, so that the end result is:

$$(1.2.3) \qquad P'(t) = -\lambda P(t),$$

which is a continuous time model of radioactive decay. From Calculus[3], we know that the solution of the equation (1.2.3) is given by the exponential function

$$P(t) = P(0)e^{-\lambda t},$$

which quantifies the familiar notion that the quantity of a radioactive material decays exponentially with time.

1.2.1. Difference equations. Discrete time models like the Fibonacci equation (1.1.1) are known as **difference equations**. Continuous time models such as the equation of radioactive decay (1.2.3) are known as **differential equations** (note the difference, ha-ha).

A general difference equation for a population model, for example, would look like this:

$$(1.2.4) \qquad x_{n+1} = f\left(x_n, x_{n-1}, \ldots, x_{n-(k-1)}\right).$$

---

[3]IMPORTANT: read §1.5.1 at the end of this chapter.

This formula tells us that we need to know the sizes of the k previous generations

$$x_n, x_{n-1}, x_{n-2}, \ldots, x_{n-(k-1)}$$

to determine what the size of the next generation is. The function f stands for whatever algebraic manipulation our model requires with this knowledge to extract x_{n+1}. The number k is known as the **order** of the difference equation. A **solution** of the equation (1.2.4) is a sequence (x_n) which satisfies it.

Fibonacci equation has order 2 – we need to know the size of two previous generations of rabbits to calculate the next one.

Of course, once we *do* know two consecutive generations x_{n-1}, x_n of Fibonacci rabbits, we can not only get x_{n+1}, but all of the following generations too (and even the previous generations, since $x_{n-1} = x_{n+1} - x_n$). More generally, for a difference equation (1.2.4), the values of k consecutive generations $x_n, x_{n-1}, \ldots, x_{n-(k-1)}$ are known as **initial data**, and once you have the initial data, you should be able to find the size of any future generation x_{n+m} even if you do not have a general formula for the solution, by repeatedly applying the recipe (1.2.4).

As for finding a general formula for x_n, starting from a difference equation (1.2.4), we have to temper our expectations. We cannot hope for it if the formula on the right-hand side of the equation is too complicated.

In both of the examples (1.1.1) and (1.2.1) we have seen so far, the expression on the right-hand side is quite simple; it is a **linear combination** of the previous values. Let us say that a difference equation is **linear** if it has the form

$$(1.2.5) \qquad x_{n+1} = a_n x_n + a_{n-1} x_{n-1} + \cdots a_{n-(k-1)} x_{n-(k-1)} + b.$$

Here the coefficients a_j and b may themselves change with n. Consider for instance the first-order linear equation

$$(1.2.6) \qquad\qquad\qquad x_{n+1} = (n+1)x_n$$

with the initial data $x_0 = 1$. Can you come up with the formula for the solution?

We say that the equation (1.2.5) is **homogeneous** if the free-standing term b is absent. Here is a very useful observation about such equations:

Theorem 1.2.1 (The Superposition Principle). *Consider a linear, homogeneous difference equation of the form*

$$x_{n+1} = a_n x_n + a_{n-1} x_{n-1} + \cdots + a_{n-(k-1)} x_{n-(k-1)}.$$

Suppose x_k^1 and x_k^2 are two different solutions of the equation (that is, two sequences, each of which satisfies the equation), and c_1 and c_2 are any coefficients. Then

$$x_k = c_1 x_k^1 + c_2 x_k^2$$

is also a solution.

As a consequence, let $x_k^1, x_k^2, \ldots, x_k^m$ be any number of solutions and $c_1, \ldots, c_m$ be any coefficients. Then

$$x_k = c_1 x_k^1 + c_2 x_k^2 + \cdots + c_m x_k^m$$

*is also a solution. To summarize, **a linear combination of solutions is again a solution.***

Proof. The proof is very easy. When we substitute $x_k = c_1 x_k^1 + c_2 x_k^2$ into the equation, we obtain

$$c_1 x_{n+1}^1 + c_2 x_{n+1}^2$$

on the left-hand side, and

$$a_n(c_1 x_n^1 + c_2 x_n^2) + a_{n-1}(c_1 x_{n-1}^1 + c_2 x_{n-1}^2) + \cdots a_{n-(k-1)}(c_1 x_{n-(k-1)}^1 + c_2 x_{n-(k-1)}^2)$$

on the right-hand side. Grouping x^1's together and factoring out c_1, and doing the same thing with x^2's and c_2, we transform the right-hand side into

$$c_1(a_n x_n^1 + a_{n-1} x_{n-1}^1 + \cdots a_{n-(k-1)} x_{n-(k-1)}^1) + c_2(a_n x_n^2 + \cdots + a_{n-(k-1)} x_{n-(k-1)}^2)$$

which clearly agrees with the left-hand side, since we have assumed that both x_k^1 and x_k^2 are solutions of the equation. $\square$

Let us further say that the linear equation (1.2.5) has **constant coefficients** if, well, all of the coefficients a_j are constants, and do not depend on n. Try saying "linear, homogeneous difference equation with constant coefficients". That is what both of our first examples (1.1.1) and (1.2.1) are like.

1.2.2. Linear (in)dependence of sequences. Let us recall that sequences

$$\{x_k^1\}_{k=0}^\infty, \{x_k^2\}_{k=0}^\infty, \ldots, \{x_k^m\}_{k=0}^\infty$$

are *linearly dependent* if there exist constants $c_1, \ldots, c_m$ which are not all equal to zero such that the linear combination

$$x_k = c_1 x_k^1 + c_2 x_k^2 + \cdots c_m x_k^m$$

is the zero sequence: $x_k = 0$ for all $k \geq 0$ (or simply $x_k \equiv 0$). The opposite of linear dependence is *linear independence*.

A relevant example. Suppose a and b are two numbers such that $a \neq b$. Then the sequences

$$x_k^1 = a^k \text{ and } x_k^2 = b^k, \; k \geq 0$$

are linearly independent. Indeed, suppose a linear combination

$$c_1 a^k + c_2 b^k \equiv 0.$$

Substituting $k = 0$ and $k = 1$ we get a system of equations

$$\begin{cases} c_1 + c_2 = 0 \\ c_1 a + c_2 b = 0 \end{cases}$$

From the first equation, $c_2 = -c_1$, so the second equation turns into

$$c_1(a - b) = 0.$$

Since $a - b \neq 0$, we have

$$c_1 = 0 \text{ and } c_2 = -c_1 = 0.$$

Generalizing the previous example. In fact, consider any collection of pairwise distinct numbers $a_1, a_2, \ldots, a_m$, $a_i \neq a_j$ if $i \neq j$. Then the sequences

$$x_k^1 = (a_1)^k, x_k^2 = (a_2)^k, \ldots, x_k^m = (a_m)^k$$

are linearly independent. The proof of this is based on a beautiful result from Linear Algebra (yes, a result from Linear Algebra can be beautiful). Suppose

$$c_1 x_k^1 + c_2 x_k^2 + \cdots c_m x_k^m \equiv 0.$$

Let us consider the first m values of k, starting from 0 and ending with $m - 1$, and let us write down the corresponding equations:

$$\begin{cases} c_1 + c_2 + \cdots + c_m = 0 \\ c_1 a_1 + c_2 a_2 + \cdots + c_m a_m = 0 \\ c_1 (a_1)^2 + c_2 (a_2)^2 + \cdots + c_m (a_m)^2 = 0 \\ \cdots \\ c_1 (a_1)^{m-1} + c_2 (a_2)^{m-1} + \cdots + c_m (a_m)^{m-1} = 0 \end{cases}$$

In the matrix form, this system of equations can be written as

(1.2.7) $$VC = 0,$$

where

$$V = \begin{pmatrix} 1 & 1 & 1 & \cdots & 1 \\ a_1 & a_2 & a_3 & \cdots & a_m \\ (a_1)^2 & (a_2)^2 & (a_3)^2 & \cdots & (a_m)^2 \\ & & \cdots & & \\ (a_1)^{m-1} & (a_2)^{m-1} & (a_3)^{m-1} & \cdots & (a_m)^{m-1} \end{pmatrix} \text{ and } C = \begin{pmatrix} c_1 \\ c_2 \\ c_3 \\ \cdots \\ c_m \end{pmatrix}$$

The matrix V is known as *Vandermonde matrix*, its determinant $|V|$ is called *Vandermonde determinant*. It turns out that $|V|$ is equal to the product of all differences $(a_j - a_i)$ where $j > i$:

$$|V| = \prod_{1 \leq i < j \leq m} (a_j - a_i).$$

Since all the terms in the product are non-zero, Vandermonde determinant is non-zero. This means that the system (1.2.7) has a unique solution $C = 0$, which implies linear independence, as advertised.

1.3. Solutions of linear difference equations

1.3.1. Solving the Fibonacci equation. It took more than 500 years until a formula for solving the Fibonacci equation appeared. It is based on an ingenious idea: let us replace x_n's by powers of some unknown variable λ in such a way, that the index n of x_n becomes the power λ^n:

$$\lambda^{n+1} = \lambda^n + \lambda^{n-1},$$

or, dividing by the smallest power of λ,

(1.3.1) $$\lambda^2 = \lambda + 1.$$

This is a quadratic equation, and it has two roots

$$\phi = \frac{1 + \sqrt{5}}{2} \text{ and } \psi = \frac{1 - \sqrt{5}}{2}.$$

Let us take one of them, for instance, ϕ, and notice that, since

$$\phi^2 = \phi + 1,$$

$$\phi^3 = \phi \cdot \phi^2 = \phi(\phi + 1) = \phi^2 + \phi,$$

$$\phi^4 = \phi(\phi^2 + \phi) = \phi^3 + \phi^2,$$

and so on. So **each power of ϕ is the sum of the previous two!** Thus, if we write $v_n = \phi^n$, then this sequence is a solution of Fibonacci equation. And since ψ is a root of the same quadratic equation, the same holds for the sequence $w_n = \psi^n$. Of course, neither one of these solutions is the Fibonacci sequence, since it does not match the initial data $x_0 = 1$, $x_1 = 1$. For instance, $v_0 = 1$ but $v_1 = \phi$. However, we can try using the Superposition Principle now, and look for the solution of the form

$$x_n = c_1 v_n + c_2 w_n.$$

Since the entire solution sequence is determined by the initial data, we only need to find the values c_1, c_2 to match $x_0 = 1, x_1 = 1$. This gives us a system of equations (for $n = 0$ and $n = 1$):

$$\begin{cases} c_1 + c_2 = 1 \\ c_1\phi + c_2\psi = 1 \end{cases}$$

Fortunately, we have the same number of equations as the unknowns, and the system is easy to solve:

$$c_1 = \frac{1 - \psi}{\phi - \psi}, \text{ and } c_2 = \frac{\phi - 1}{\phi - \psi},$$

so

$$x_n = \frac{(1 - \psi)\phi^n + (\phi - 1)\psi^n}{\phi - \psi}.$$

Noting that $1 - \psi = \phi$ and $\phi - 1 = -\psi$, we get an expression that is easy to remember:

$$x_n = \frac{\phi^{n+1} - \psi^{n+1}}{\phi - \psi} = \frac{\phi^{n+1} - \psi^{n+1}}{\sqrt{5}},$$

which is commonly known as *Binet's formula*.

Of the two roots of (1.3.1), $|\phi| > 1$ and $|\psi| < 1$, so in the formula for x_n for large values of n the power ϕ^n will dominate, and this means that Fibonacci rabbit population grows "like" the power law:

$$x_n \sim \text{const} \cdot \phi^n.$$

The number ϕ is special, it has been known since ancient times as **the golden ratio**. In art and architecture, proportions whose ratio is the golden ratio are supposedly the most pleasing to the eye. It is amusing to note that Fibonacci himself was definitely familiar with the golden ratio, and the "magic" formula $\phi^2 = \phi + 1$, but it took another five centuries for the formula for the Fibonacci sequence to be discovered.

We can now substitute $n = 12$ into the formula to obtain $x_{12} = 233$, which solves the original Fibonacci's problem. And yes, it would have been easier to do it by hand, by a repeated application of Fibonacci equation (1.1.1). But the beauty of having the formula is that it can be applied for any n with equal ease (well, we do need to use a computer to calculate the roots and the powers involved). For instance, x_{382} is equal to [4]:

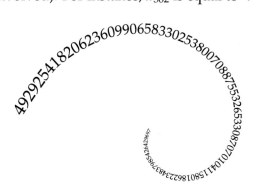

Good luck computing that by hand!

1.3.2. We have solved one equation. What about all the others?
The trick we have just seen can be easily generalized. Let us look at **any**
second-order homogeneous equation with constant coefficients:

(1.3.2)
$$x_{n+1} = \alpha x_n + \beta x_{n-1},$$

and replace k-th x with the k-th power of λ, as before:

$$\lambda^{n+1} = \alpha \lambda^n + \beta \lambda^{n-1},$$

which is the same as

(1.3.3)
$$\lambda^2 = \alpha \lambda + \beta.$$

This equation is known as **the characteristic equation** of our difference
equation. Remember this name, we will see it often.

Since it is a quadratic equation, it has either one or two roots. To begin
with, let us assume that there are two roots λ_1 and λ_2. Similarly to what
we have seen with Fibonacci sequence, $v_n = (\lambda_1)^n$ and $w_n = (\lambda_2)^n$ are
solutions of our equation. Indeed,

$$v_2 = (\lambda_1)^2 = \alpha(\lambda_1)^1 + \beta(\lambda_1)^0 = \alpha v_1 + \beta v_0,$$

$$v_3 = (\lambda_1)^3 = \lambda_1 \cdot (\lambda_1)^2 = \alpha(\lambda_1)^2 + \beta(\lambda_1)^1 = \alpha v_2 + \beta v_1, \text{ etc.}$$

To turn this observation into a rigorous proof by induction, let us assume
that

$$v_n = (\lambda_1)^n = \alpha(\lambda_1)^{n-1} + \beta(\lambda_1)^{n-2} = \alpha v_{n-1} + \beta v_{n-2}, \text{ then}$$

---

[4]Just for the fun of it, since this number would not fit on the page, I bent it into the *golden spiral*:
another familiar mathematical object associated with the Fibonacci sequence.

$$v_{n+1} = (\lambda_1)^{n+1} = \lambda_1 \cdot (\lambda_1)^n = \alpha(\lambda_1)^n + \beta(\lambda_1)^{n-1} = \alpha v_n + \beta v_{n-1},$$

which is what we needed to demonstrate.

Of course, the same holds for $w_n = (\lambda_2)^n$. We thus obtain two different sequences of solutions: $v_n = (\lambda_1)^n$ and $w_n = (\lambda_2)^n$. Using the Superposition Principle, we can now match any initial data using the solution

(1.3.4) $$x_n = c_1 v_n + c_2 w_n,$$

with appropriately chosen coefficients c_1, c_2. For instance, if we are given the values of x_0 and x_1 as initial data, then we can find c_1, c_2 from the equations:

(1.3.5) $$\begin{cases} c_1 + c_2 = x_0 \\ c_1\lambda_1 + c_2\lambda_2 = x_1 \end{cases}$$

(but of course, any other initial data would do). If you are a fan of Linear Algebra, you will be pleased to observe that the determinant of the above system of linear equations is $\lambda_2 - \lambda_1 \neq 0$, so it has a unique solution.

Let us introduce a bit more terminology. The formula (1.3.4) represents the **general solution** of the difference equation (1.3.2). The general solution is a linear combination of two linearly independent solutions v_n and w_n (hello Linear Algebra again). We say that it is a **two-parameter family** of sequences, with a pair of **undetermined (or free) parameters** c_1 and c_2. The values of the parameters can be pinned down using the initial data. The equation (1.3.2) *together* with initial data form an **initial value problem**. The unique solution of this problem, obtained by solving the system (1.3.5) is called **a particular solution**. We will use this terminology routinely, you should memorize it!

Of course, there remains the unpleasant possibility that the characteristic equation has only one (multiple) root:

$$\lambda_1 = \lambda_2.$$

The above method no longer works, since we would only produce one solution sequence $v_n = (\lambda_1)^n$. Let us verify that we can get the second solution in this case as

$$w_n = n(\lambda_1)^n.$$

Before we do that, let us factor the polynomial $\lambda^2 - \alpha\lambda - \beta$ as

(1.3.6) $$\lambda^2 - \alpha\lambda - \beta = (\lambda - \lambda_1)^2,$$

and note that this implies that

$$\lambda_1 = \frac{\alpha}{2}.$$

Now, let us set

$$w_n = n(\lambda_1)^n,$$

and see if we can verify that

$$w_{n+1} = \alpha w_n + \beta w_{n-1}.$$

When we substitute the formula for w_n into the right-hand side of the above equation, we obtain

$$\alpha n(\lambda_1)^n + \beta(n-1)(\lambda_1)^{n-1} = \alpha(\lambda_1)^n + (n-1)[\alpha(\lambda_1)^n + \beta(\lambda_1)^{n-1}].$$

From the characteristic equation, the expression in square brackets is equal to $(\lambda_1)^{n+1}$, so the right-hand side becomes

$$\alpha(\lambda_1)^n + (n-1)(\lambda_1)^{n+1}.$$

Since $\alpha = 2\lambda_1$, this is equal to

$$2\lambda_1 \cdot (\lambda_1)^n + (n-1)(\lambda_1)^{n+1} = (n+1)(\lambda_1)^{n+1},$$

which is what we needed to prove.

So in the case when λ_1 is the only root, we can write any solution as

$$x_n = c_1(\lambda_1)^n + c_2 n(\lambda_1)^n$$

where c_1, c_2 can be found from the initial data.

We have thus learned how to solve **any** linear homogeneous equation of order 2 with constant coefficients!

One more thing, before we go on. It can, of course happen that the characteristic equation (1.3.1) has two complex conjugate roots

$$\lambda = a \pm ib.$$

Then the two solutions $v_n = (a+ib)^n$ and $w_n = (a-ib)^n$ will both be complex. Since the initial data are real, this means that the constants c_1 and c_2 will be such that the imaginary parts of $c_1 v_n$ and $c_2 w_n$ cancel, so that x_n only has real values. This is not a problem, of course. However, if you prefer not to deal with complex numbers, here is a workaround.

Write the roots in the polar form (well, you do need to know *something* about complex numbers):

$$\lambda_1 = r(\cos\theta + i\sin\theta) \text{ and } \lambda_2 = r(\cos\theta - i\sin\theta).$$

By de Moivre's formula,

$$v_n = (\lambda_1)^n = r^n(\cos(n\theta) + i\sin(n\theta)) \text{ and } w_n = (\lambda_2)^n = r^n(\cos(n\theta) - i\sin(n\theta)).$$

Now, recall the Superposition Principle: any linear combination of solutions is again a solution. In particular, this is true for

$$y_n = \frac{v_n + w_n}{2} = r^n\cos(n\theta) \text{ and } z_n = \frac{v_n - w_n}{2i} = r^n\sin(n\theta).$$

The sequences y_n and z_n are, of course, real – and we can now look for the solution of the form

$$x_n = d_1 y_n + d_2 z_n = d_1 r^n\cos(n\theta) + d_2 r^n\sin(n\theta).$$

You may prefer this workaround in practice, since it eliminates the need to work with complex numbers when finding the values of the parameters in a particular solution.

1.3.3. General solutions of linear homogeneous difference equations with constant coefficients of an arbitrary order. Wow, that was a mouthful... Anyway, generalizing from order 2 to order k is fairly straightforward.

Suppose we are given a difference equation of the form

(1.3.7) $\qquad x_{n+1} = a_{k-1}x_n + a_{k-2}x_{n-1} + \cdots a_0 x_{n-(k-1)}.$

Replacing each x_j with a power λ^j we obtain the equation:

$$\lambda^{n+1} = a_{k-1}\lambda^n + a_{k-2}\lambda^{n-1} + \cdots + a_0\lambda^{n-(k-1)}.$$

After dividing by $\lambda^{n-(k-1)}$ we get a polynomial equation of order k:

(1.3.8) $\qquad \lambda^k = a_{k-1}\lambda^{k-1} + a_{k-2}\lambda^{k-2} + \cdots + a_1\lambda + a_0,$

or (bringing all of the λ's to the left-hand side)

$$\lambda^k - a_{k-1}\lambda^{k-1} - a_{k-2}\lambda^{k-2} - \cdots - a_1\lambda - a_0 = 0$$

which is the characteristic equation of (1.3.7). The characteristic equation has k roots[5] $\lambda_1,\ldots,\lambda_k$ which can be real or complex, and some of which can be repeated; so the polynomial

$$P(\lambda) = \lambda^k - a_{k-1}\lambda^{k-1} - a_{k-2}\lambda^{k-2} - \cdots - a_1\lambda - a_0$$

[5]See §1.5.2

factors as

(1.3.9) $$P(\lambda) = (\lambda - \lambda_1)(\lambda - \lambda_2) \cdots (\lambda - \lambda_k).$$

Note, that the complex roots will come in conjugate pairs:

(1.3.10) $$\lambda = a \pm ib = r(\cos \theta \pm i \sin \theta).$$

Theorem 1.3.1. *Given the equation (1.3.7), suppose λ_j is a root of the characteristic equation (1.3.8) which is repeated m times in the product (1.3.9). Then, we obtain m solution sequences:*

$$v_{1,n} = (\lambda_j)^n,$$
$$v_{2,n} = n(\lambda_j)^n,$$
$$v_{3,n} = n^2(\lambda_j)^n,$$
$$\cdots$$
$$v_{m,n} = n^{m-1}(\lambda_j)^n.$$

The general solution is a linear combination of all such sequences obtained from each root λ_j.

Since a root repeated m times produces exactly m sequences, and the product (1.3.9) has exactly k linear factors, the general solution will be a k-parameter family. The initial data can be used to pin down the values of the parameters and obtain a particular solution.

For complex conjugate roots we can modify this procedure as before. Suppose we have a pair of complex conjugate roots (1.3.10), each of which is repeated m times (so together they account for $2m$ factors in (1.3.9). Then, we can use the following $2m$ solution sequences:

$$y_{l,n} = n^l r^n \cos(n\theta) \text{ and } z_{l,n} = n^l r^n \sin(n\theta) \text{ for } l = 0, 1, \ldots, m-1.$$

1.3.4. Example: equations of order 1.

$$x_{n+1} = ax_n.$$

We do not really need any general theory to tell us what will result from repeated multiplications by a constant a:

$$x_n = a^n x_0.$$

In fact, we have already seen this example when we discussed radioactive decay. However, let us still solve the equation following the general recipe. The characteristic equation is

$$\lambda = a,$$

it has a single root a, and therefore the general solution is... well, you guessed it,
$$x_n = ca^n,$$
and the parameter c can be found by setting $n = 0$ to be $c = x_0$.

1.3.5. One more example.
$$x_n = 6x_{n-1} - 9x_{n-2}, \ x_0 = 1, \ x_1 = 0.$$
The equation has order 2 and the characteristic equation is
$$\lambda^2 = 6\lambda - 9, \text{ or } \lambda^2 - 6\lambda + 9 = 0.$$
It has a single root $\lambda = 3$, so the general solution has the form
$$x_n = c_1 3^n + c_2 n 3^n = 3^n(c_1 + nc_2).$$
Substituting the initial data we get
$$c_1 = 1 \text{ and } 3(c_1 + c_2) = 0,$$
so $c_2 = -1$. Hence, the solution is
$$x_n = 3^n(1 - n).$$

1.3.6. And another example.
$$x_{n+1} = -8x_{n-1} - 16x_{n-3}.$$
This is a slightly more challenging example. The order of the equation is 4, and the characteristic equation is
$$\lambda^4 = -8\lambda^2 - 16, \text{ or } \lambda^4 + 8\lambda^2 + 16 = 0.$$
This factors as
$$(\lambda^2 + 4)^2 = (\lambda + 2i)^2(\lambda - 2i)^2 = 0,$$
so we get two roots,
$$\lambda = 2i = 2\left(\cos\frac{\pi}{2} + i\sin\frac{\pi}{2}\right), \text{ and } \lambda = -2i = 2\left(\cos\frac{\pi}{2} - i\sin\frac{\pi}{2}\right).$$
We can thus write the general solution as
$$(1.3.11) \qquad x_n = c_1(2i)^n + c_2 n(2i)^n + c_3(-2i)^n + c_4 n(-2i)^n,$$
which is a 4-parameter family, and so we need four successive values of the sequence as initial data. Now, if we look at the original equation more closely, we will see that if the index n is even on the left, then the two indices on the right: $n - 2$, $n - 4$ are also even, and the same is true for the

odd-values of the indices. So, we should be able to determine all succes-sive even-numbered x's from two consecutive even numbered values, for instance x_0 and x_2. And knowing x_1, x_3 should suffice to determine all odd-numbered x's. Indeed, if we plug in an even value $n = 2l$ into (1.3.11), then, since $i^{2l} = (-1)^l$, we obtain

$$x_{2l} = (-1)^l 2^{2l}[(c_1 + c_3) + 2l(c_2 + c_4)].$$

Similarly, if $n = 2l + 1$, we obtain

$$x_{2l+1} = i(-1)^l 2^{2l+1}[(c_1 - c_3) + (2l + 1)(c_2 - c_4)].$$

Note the imaginary unit in front of the second expression. Since the values of x_n are real, this is only possible if both $c_1 - c_3$ and $c_2 - c_4$ are imaginary. And, of course, in the previous equation, the expressions $c_1 + c_3$ and $c_2 + c_4$ must be real. This means that if

$$c_1 = a_1 + ib_1, \text{ and } c_2 = a_2 + ib_2, \text{ then}$$

$$c_3 = a_1 - ib_1, \text{ and } c_4 = a_2 - ib_2.$$

Thus,

$$x_{2l} = (-1)^l 2^{2l}[2a_1 + 2l \cdot 2a_2] \text{ and } x_{2l+1} = (-1)^{l+1} 2^{2l+1}[2b_1 + (2l + 1) \cdot 2b_2],$$

so indeed, we only need two free real parameters to determine all of the even-numbered values of x_n, and the same is true for the odd-numbered values.

Finally, in this example we could have used the polar form of the roots, and write the general solution as

$$x_n = d_1 2^n \cos \frac{n\pi}{2} + d_2 2^n \sin \frac{n\pi}{2} + d_3 n 2^n \cos \frac{n\pi}{2} + d_4 n 2^n \sin \frac{n\pi}{2}.$$

For even values of n the sines will vanish in the above formula, and for odd values of n the cosines will vanish, so we see that

$$x_{2l} = 2^{2l} \cos(\pi l)(d_1 + 2ld_3) \text{ and } x_{2l+1} = 2^{2l_1} \sin \frac{(2l + 1)\pi}{2}(d_2 + (2l + 1)d_4).$$

1.3.7. A more realistic rabbit population. Fibonacci rabbits never die, which is not a very realistic scenario. Let us tweak the model by intro-ducing two survival rates: α for adult rabbits, and β for the newborns. For good measure, let us also throw in a fertitlity parameter γ, which will represent the average number of newborn rabbit pairs each breeding pair produces per month. The assumption that rabbits are born in male/female pairs is not particularly realistic either, but is not very relevant, we can simply assume that x_n is the number of adult female rabbits in each generation and not count the males.

If we let y_n represent the number of newborn females, then we obtain the following two equations:

$$(1.3.12) \qquad \begin{cases} x_{n+1} = \alpha x_n + \beta y_n \\ y_{n+1} = \gamma \alpha x_n \end{cases}$$

This is our first example of a **system** of difference equations, we will be seeing lots of those. From these two equations we obtain a modified Fibonacci model:

$$(1.3.13) \qquad x_{n+1} = \alpha x_n + \beta \gamma \alpha x_{n-1}.$$

 Maple **code for the sequence (1.3.13).**
To begin with, here is a very basic code for generating the sequence x_n with *Maple* (I used Latin letters for the parameters, instead of Greek ones):

```
>xn:=proc(n):
 if n=1 then return a1:
 elif n=2 then return a2:
 else return a*xn(n-1)+b*g*a*xn(n-2):
 end if;
 end proc;
```

A pro tip: use Shift-Enter instead of Enter when you want to enter a multi-line command.

Note that just like the equation (1.3.13), this code is *recursive*: it calls on itself for the previous terms in the sequence.

Let us arbitrarily select some values for the parameters:

```
>a1:=100;a2:=90;a:=0.55;b:=0.4;g:=2;
```

We can now calculate several consecutive terms in the sequence. For instance,

```
>xn(7);xn(8);
```

outputs 89.746..., 89.054.... The population seems to be slowly decreasing. To check this, let us solve the characteristic equation:

```
>char:=x^2=a*x+b*g*a;
>fsolve(char);
```

Maple outputs the roots:

```
-0.4430703308, 0.9930703308
```

And we can see that moduli of both of the roots are less than 1, so the population will, indeed, decrease with time.

Finally, the command **rsolve** in *Maple* can be used to get an exact formula for the roots of a difference equation ("r" in "rsolve" stands for "recursion"):

```
>rsolve(x(n+1)=a*x(n)+b*g*a*x(n-1),x(k));
```
   will output an algebraic formula for $x(n)$.

1.3.8. Some more about Fibonacci numbers. Since medieval times, the golden ratio and Fibonacci sequence were frequently "observed" in nature. Most of these observations are, of course, somewhat speculative. One such speculation concerns the dimensions of the human hand. It is thought that "ideal" proportions of the phalanges (bones of human fingers) grow by approximately the golden ratio. A possible explanation of this observation is that their lengths follow the Fibonacci rules: in the notation of Figure 5,

$$A + B = C, \text{ and } B + C = D.$$

This becomes quite believable if we think of how the phalanges fold together when we clench the hand into a fist (Figure 5 (c)). A similar rule

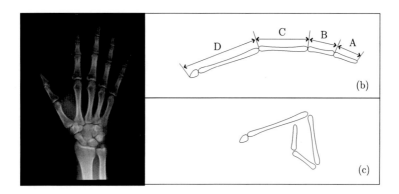

Figure 5. (a) an X-ray of a human hand; (b) the phalanges of a single finger; (c) the same phalanges in a closed hand.

is thought to be obeyed by successive tailbones of some animals, such as chameleons.

If we imagine that aliens on planet XYZ have evolved hands in which *three*, rather than two phalanges fold into one when the fist is clenched, then the sequence of lengths will obey the law:

(1.3.14) $$x_{n+1} = x_n + x_{n-1} + x_{n-2},$$

which is sometimes called **tribonacci** rule. The tribonacci sequence is obtained by starting with the initial data:

$$x_0 = x_1 = 0, \ x_2 = 1.$$

1.4. Non-homogeneous equations

Here is a real-life example. Suppose you have a savings account, and the bank charges you (the way banks often do) a flat monthly fee for the priviledge of keeping your money there. Let us assume that the bank also pays interest on your deposit, which is accrued monthly, so in the absence of any fees, our principal P_t at the end of the t-th month would grow as

$$(1.4.1) \qquad\qquad P_{t+1} = aP_t$$

for some $a > 1$. With the subtraction of r dollars at the end of each month, the difference equation takes the form

$$(1.4.2) \qquad\qquad P_{t+1} = aP_t - r$$

This is a non-homogeneous equation. It is not completely trivial to solve because even though the amount we subtract every month is the same, the effect of these amounts is not equal. The earlier the fee is subtracted, the more damage it does to the future growth of the account (can you explain why?)

If we start with P_0 in the account, then

$$
\begin{aligned}
P_1 &= aP_0 - r, \\
P_2 &= aP_1 - r = a^2 P_0 - ar - r, \\
P_3 &= aP_2 - r = a^3 P_0 - a^2 r - ar - r, \\
&\cdots \\
P_n &= a^n P_0 - a^{n-1}r - a^{n-2}r - \cdots - a^2 r - ar - r \\
&= a^n P_0 - (a^{n-1} + a^{n-2} + \cdots + a^2 + a + 1)r.
\end{aligned}
$$

Using the formula for the sum of the geometric progression[6], we can rewrite this as

$$(1.4.3) \qquad\qquad P_n = a^n P_0 - \frac{a^n - 1}{a - 1} r.$$

Here is a general theorem, which applies to equations of this sort:

---

[6]The formula for $S = 1 + a + a^2 + \cdots + a^{n-1}$ is difficult (at least for me) to memorize; it is much easier, and more fun, to see that $aS = S - 1 + a^n$, and solve for S.

Theorem 1.4.1 (General solution of a non-homogeneous equation). *Consider a linear, non-homogeneous difference equation with constant coefficients [a] of the form*

(1.4.4) $\qquad x_{n+1} = a_n x_n + a_{n-1} x_{n-1} + \cdots + a_{n-(k-1)} x_{n-(k-1)} + b.$

Consider the corresponding homogeneous equation (which is obtained by dropping the b term):

(1.4.5) $\qquad x_{n+1} = a_n x_n + a_{n-1} x_{n-1} + \cdots + a_{n-(k-1)} x_{n-(k-1)},$

and let

$$x_n^h = c_1 v_{1,n} + c_2 v_{2,n} + \cdots + c_k v_{k,n}$$

be its general solution.

   Now suppose x_n^{nh} is any solution of the original non-homogeneous equation (1.4.4)[b]. Then its general solution is given by

$$x_n = x_n^h + x_n^{nh}.$$

---

[a]Here b does not have to be a constant, it can depend on n, so it would be properly written as b_n. This would not change the conclusion of the theorem.

[b]For no particular reason, such a solution is called **a particular solution**

So, for instance, the solution (1.4.3) is a combination of the term $a^n P_0$, which is the general solution of the homogeneous equation (1.4.1), and the sequence $-\frac{a^n-1}{a-1}r$, which is a particular solution of (1.4.2).

The difficulty in applying Theorem 1.4.1 should be clear. We have a very detailed recipe for finding x_n^h, however, there is no prescription in the statement of the theorem on how to find any sequence x_n^{nh} which would satisfy the non-homogeneous equation. So it is not that easy to produce another natural example of a non-homogeneous equation for which a particular solution would be easy to find.

1.5. Some concluding remarks

1.5.1. Why is $(e^x)' = e^x$? It is obviously a silly question – because it says so on the inside cover of any Calculus textbook! But what if you actually had to derive this rule? What would you need to know about the exponential function?

Wait, let us take a step back – before talking about the exponential *function*, what if you are simply asked to evaluate the number e itself? After all, if you cannot compute $e = e^1$ you can hardly hope to say something about e^x in the general case. And while e^1 can be computed by pressing a button on a calculator, or even asking your phone, someone at some point had to figure out a way to compute its value (and "teach" the calculator to do it).

These questions apply not just to the exponential function, but pretty much to any other "elementary" function you know. Take trigonometric functions, for example. How would you calclulate $\sin(1)$? The value 1 here stands for one radian, of course, which is the angle which cuts out the arc of length 1 on the unit circle. Just imagine having to measure such an angle accurately, then putting it in a right triangle, then measuring the opposite side and the hypotenuse, and finally taking their ratio... This cannot possibly be what my calculator is doing when it outputs

$$\sin(1) \approx 0.841470...,$$

right? Hopefully, by now, you know what actually needs to be done. As you have learned in Calculus, elementary functions can be represented as sums of their Taylor series. For $\sin(x)$, $\cos(x)$, and e^x, it is most convenient to use the Taylor series at the origin. For the sine function it looks as follows:

$$(1.5.1) \qquad \sin(x) = x - \frac{x^3}{3!} + \frac{x^5}{5!} - \frac{x^7}{7!} + \cdots = \sum_{k=0}^{\infty} (-1)^k \frac{x^{2k+1}}{(2k+1)!}.$$

If I plug in $x = 1$, and use only the first few terms of the series, I get

$$\sin(1) \approx 1 - \frac{1}{6} + \frac{1}{120} \approx 0.84166...$$

Not a bad approximation at all, for a couple of minutes' work!

It is a great idea to think of these series as *the definitions* of elementary functions. They are much more useful than the other "definitions" you have learned, because you can actually use them to compute the values of the functions, and more. Thus,

$$(1.5.2) \qquad \cos(x) = 1 - \frac{x^2}{2!} + \frac{x^4}{4!} - \frac{x^6}{6!} + \cdots = \sum_{k=0}^{\infty} (-1)^k \frac{x^{2k}}{(2k)!},$$

(remember that $0! = 1$) and

$$(1.5.3) \qquad e^x = 1 + x + \frac{x^2}{2!} + \frac{x^3}{3!} + \frac{x^4}{4!} + \cdots = \sum_{n=0}^{\infty} \frac{x^n}{n!}.$$

We can easily derive

$$\frac{d}{dt} e^{at} = a e^{at}$$

by substituting $x = at$ and differentiating the sum (1.5.3) term by term:

$$(1.5.4) \qquad \begin{aligned} \frac{d}{dt}(e^{at}) &= \frac{d}{dt}\left(1 + at + \frac{a^2 t^2}{2!} + \frac{a^3 t^3}{3!} + \frac{a^4 t^4}{4!} + \cdots\right) \\ &= 0 + a + 2\frac{a^2 t}{2!} + 3\frac{a^3 t^2}{3!} + 4\frac{a^4 t^3}{4!} + \cdots \\ &= a\left(1 + at + \frac{a^2 t^2}{2!} + \frac{a^3 t^3}{3!} + \cdots\right) = a e^{at}. \end{aligned}$$

We can verify all of the usual properties of elementary functions. For instance,

$$\sin(-x) = -\sin(x);$$

since the series (1.5.1) only has odd powers of x in it, and $(-x)^{2k+1} = -x^{2k+1}$ (and, incidentally this is why such functions are called "odd" functions). Try checking

$$e^{x+y} = e^x e^y,$$

it is a good exercise.

These definitions can be applied with an equal ease to complex values of the argument. For instance, if we plug in an imaginary number iy into the series (1.5.3) for the exponential, we will obtain

$$e^{iy} = 1 + iy + \frac{i^2 y^2}{2!} + \frac{i^3 y^3}{3!} + \frac{i^4 y^4}{4!} + \cdots.$$

Using $i^2 = -1$, and separating the real and the imaginary parts, we get

$$e^{iy} = \left(1 - \frac{y^2}{2!} + \frac{y^4}{4!} - \cdots\right) + i\left(y - \frac{y^3}{3!} + \frac{y^5}{5!} - \cdots\right) = \cos(y) + i\sin(y).$$

This is the famous **Euler's formula**. For a general complex number $z = x + iy$ we then get

$$e^z = e^x e^{iy} = e^x(\cos(y) + i\sin(y)).$$

If we raise e^{iy} to a power n, we will get

$$(e^{iy})^n = (\cos(y) + i\sin(y))^n = e^{iny} = \cos(ny) + i\sin(ny),$$

which is the (also famous) **de Moivre's formula**.

We can even plug in matrices rather than numbers into these definitions. For instance, for a square $n \times n$ matrix A, we can set

$$(1.5.5) \qquad e^A = \sum_{n=0}^{\infty} \frac{A^n}{n!} = I + A + \frac{A^2}{2!} + \frac{A^3}{3!} + \cdots,$$

known as the **matrix exponential**. And pretending that $a = A$ in the calculation (1.5.4), we get

$$(1.5.6) \qquad \frac{d}{dt}e^{tA} = Ae^{tA}.$$

1.5.2. Note: it can be difficult to find the roots of a characteristic equation. Everyone is familiar with the "quadratic formula" for the roots of a quadratic equation

$$a\lambda^2 + b\lambda + c = 0.$$

It is less widely known, that there is a general formula for the roots of a cubic equation

$$a\lambda^3 + b\lambda^2 + c\lambda + d = 0.$$

The derivation of this formula was a great triumph of Renaissance mathematics of early 16th century (and a focus of much scientific rivalry of that time). The "cubic formula" is not taught at school alongside the quadratic one for two reasons: firstly, it is quite cumbersome and difficult to memorize, and secondly, using it requires manipulations with complex numbers (which may be required even if all three roots of the cubic are real). The discovery of the formula for the roots of a general equation of degree 4 followed soon after – and it is, of course, even scarier. But still, it is explicit, and can be taught to a computer without any difficulty.

The situation changes radically for equations of degree 5 and higher:

There does not exist an algebraic[7] formula for solving a general polynomial equation of degree $n \geq 5$.

---

[7]An algebraic formula for the roots is a formula involving only the coefficients of the polynomial, the four arithmetic operations, and roots of an integer degree.

This is a theorem, whose proof was given by Niels Henrik Abel in 1824 (incidentally, the Nobel Prize equivalent for mathematicians is the Abel Prize).

So, in general, given a polynomial equation of a degree larger than 4, such as the characteristic equation of a difference equation of order larger than 4, its roots cannot be known *exactly*. There exist numerous techniques for finding the roots approximately, starting with the Newton's Method which you may have seen in your Calculus course. In fact, the problem of polynomial root finding is one of the most practically important problems in mathematics, and there is a great interest in developing root-finding algorithms.

There is, however, an objective difficulty with trying to approximate the roots of a polynomial numerically: their positions can change dramatically with a very small change in the coefficients of the polynomial. Here is a simple to understand example. Consider the polynomial

$$\lambda^{10} = 0.$$

It only has a single root, of course, $\lambda = 0$. Next, let us subtract 10^{-10} on the left-hand side. One of the roots of the polynomial

$$\lambda^{10} - 10^{-10} = 0$$

is $\lambda = 0.1$, which is very much not zero. Now, 10^{-10} is a decimal dot followed by nine zeros and then a one. Most calculators will simply not distinguish this number from zero, so numerically, there is hardly any difference between the first and the second polynomials. However, the roots are quite different. This simple observation seriously complicates the situation with numerical root finding. At the very least, you should treat the values of any roots output by a computer with a great deal of caution, even if they *seem* to fit the equation quite well.

**Exercises for
Chapter 1**

1. Solve the equation 1.2.6 with the initial data $x_0 = 1$.

2. **(practice makes perfect)** Find the general solution of each of the following difference equations:
   (a) $x_{n+2} = 4x_{n+1} - 3x_n$,
   (b) $x_{n+1} = -4x_n - 8x_{n-1}$,
   (c) $x_{n+2} = 3x_{n+1} - 3x_n + x_{n-1}$.

3. **(and more practice)**
   (a) Find the solution of the equation (a) from Problem 2 with initial data $x_0 = 1$, $x_1 = 2$.
   (b) Find the solution of the equation (b) from Problem 2 with initial data $x_0 = 1$, $x_1 = 1$.
   (c) Find the solution of the equation (c) from Problem 2 with initial data $x_0 = x_1 = 1$, $x_2 = -1$.

4. Consider the Fibonacci rabbit population with harvesting: every month starting with the third one, two pairs rabbits, starting with the youngest, are removed from the field. Write the difference equation for this population. Find the number of pairs in the field after 12 months.

5. Consider the equation

$$x_{n+1} = x_n + x_{n-1} - x_{n-2}.$$

   (a) Find the general solution (you will need to guess a root of the characteristic equation).
   (b) Find the solution which agrees with $x_0 = 1$, $x_1 = 1$, $x_2 = 2$.

6. **(a "proof" problem, just for the fun of it)** Let S_n be the number of ways you can climb n stairs while taking either one or two stairs at a time. For instance, you can climb 3 stairs in 3 different ways: $1 - 1 - 1$, $1 - 2$, $2 - 1$, and thus $S_3 = 3$. Show that the numbers S_n satisfy the Fibonacci equation

$$S_n = S_{n-1} + S_{n-2}.$$

7. Consider the difference equation

$$x_{n+1} = x_n + x_{n-1} + x_{n-2}$$

   defined by the tribonacci rule.
   (a) Write down the characteristic equation.
   (b) The characteristic equation has three distinct roots. Denote them ϕ, ψ, θ and find the general solution.
   (c) Use the tribonacci initial conditions $x_0 = x_1 = 0, x_2 = 1$ to find the formula for x_n (in terms of ϕ, ψ, θ).
   (d) Use a computer algebra system to find the approximate values for the roots ϕ, ψ, θ, and substitute them into the formula for x_n to find the tribonacci number x_{12}.
   (e) What is the limit of x_{n+1}/x_n as $n \longrightarrow \infty$?

8. Solve the difference equation

$$P_n = aP_{n-1} - r$$

   with the given values of parameters:
   (a) $a = \frac{1}{4}, r = 1$ and initial data $P_0 = 1$.
   (b) $a = 2, r = \frac{1}{4}$ and initial data $P_0 = \frac{1}{2}$.

9. Find the general solution of the difference equation $x_n = x_{n-1} - r$.

10. ⊙ Solve the difference equation $x_n = x_{n-2} + 4$ with initial data $x_0 = 1, x_1 = 3$.

11. Calculate $e^{\begin{pmatrix} 0 & 1 & 0 \\ 0 & 0 & 1 \\ 0 & 0 & 0 \end{pmatrix}}$.

12. Suppose that Fibonacci rabbits live only three months.
   (a) Calculate the first four terms of the sequence x_n starting with $x_0 = 1, x_1 = 1$.
   (b) ⊙ Verify the equation

$$x_{n+4} = x_{n+3} + x_{n+2} - x_n.$$

   (c) Use the equation to find x_8.

Modeling with systems of difference equations

2.1. Stage-structured population models

2.1.1. Setting the stage. In most population models, it makes sense to divide the population into several age groups, known as **stages**, which differ by their mortality, fertility, etc. As a simple example of a **stage-structured** population model, have another look at the model (1.3.12), in which only two stages are present: newborns and adults. They have different survival rates, and different fertility. A stage-structured model is naturally described by a system of several equations – one for the evolution of each stage.

As an instructive example, consider the model of the population of loggerhead turtles from Crouse et. al. **[Cro87]**. Their development naturally splits into seven different stages, as seen in the table below. The stages have varying habits, which leads to a different set of dangers and therefore different survival rates. The turtles are fertile only in the last three stages of their lives, with rather different fertility rates (as usual, in these models we only consider female turtles).

Number	Stage	Ages	Annual survival rate	Eggs laid per year
1	eggs, hatchlings	<1	0.6747	0
2	small juveniles	1-7	0.7857	0
3	large juveniles	8-15	0.6758	0
4	subadults	16-21	0.7425	0
5	novice breeders	22	0.8091	127
6	remigrants	23	0.8091	4
7	mature breeders	24-54	0.8091	80

Let us denote the number of turtles at j-th stage in year n by $x_{j,n}$. We need 7 equations to describe this model. The first one is the easiest, it describes the number of new eggs laid each year, and (look at the last column in the table) is given by

$$x_{1,n+1} = 127x_{5,n} + 4x_{6,n} + 80x_{7,n}.$$

To write the rest of the equations, we have to figure out the annual contribution to each stage coming from all stages which actually contribute to it.

Suppose we would like to know what proportion of small juveniles (stage 2) become large juveniles (stage 3) each year, and what proportion remains at stage 2. Stage 2 lasts 6 years – from age 1 to age 7. Let us assume that the numbers of small juveniles of each age *are relatively stable from year to year* – a sensible assumption in a well-established population. Since the annual survival rate is $p = 0.7857$, we will have $p = 0.7857$ times fewer 2-year olds as 1-year olds, p^2 times fewer 3-year olds than 1-year olds, and the numbers will go down annually, so that there are only $p^6 \approx 0.2352$ times as many 7-year olds as 1-year olds. Thus, the total population of stage 2 (which is composed of $1 - 7$-year olds) is

$$\text{(number of one-year olds)} \quad \times \quad (1 + p + p^2 + p^3 + p^4 + p^5 + p^6)$$
$$\approx \text{(number of one-year olds)} \quad \times \quad 3.8038,$$

which we can calculate either by brute force or using the formula for the sum of a geometric progression. The number of 8-year olds is, of course

$$\text{(number of one-year olds)} \times p^7 \approx \text{(number of one-year olds)} \times 0.1848.$$

So the fraction of small juveniles who become large juveniles each year is

$$\frac{\text{number of eight-year olds}}{\text{number of all small juveniles}} \approx \frac{0.1848}{3.8038} \approx 0.0486.$$

We can similarly calculate the fraction of stage 2 which will survive and remain in stage 2 each year as

$$\frac{(\text{number of } 1 - 6\text{-year olds}) \times p}{\text{number of all small juveniles}} \approx 0.7370.$$

Thus, $0.0486x_{2,n}$ will go towards $x_{3,n+1}$, and $0.7370x_{2,n}$ will contribute to $x_{2,n+1}$.

Doing this with the whole table, gives the following system of equations:

(2.1.1)

$$\begin{cases} x_{1,n+1} = 127x_{5,n} + 4x_{6,n} + 80x_{7,n} \\[2mm] x_{2,n+1} = 0.6747x_{1,n} + 0.7370x_{2,n} \\[2mm] x_{3,n+1} = 0.0486x_{2,n} + 0.6610x_{3,n} \\[2mm] x_{4,n+1} = 0.0147x_{3,n} + 0.6907x_{4,n} \\[2mm] x_{5,n+1} = 0.0518x_{4,n} \\[2mm] x_{6,n+1} = 0.8091x_{5,n} \\[2mm] x_{7,n+1} = 0.8091x_{6,n} + 0.8089x_{7,n} \end{cases}$$

As is usual with linear systems of equations, this system will look much neater if we write it in a matrix form. To do this, let us introduce a column vector

$$X_n = \begin{pmatrix} x_{1,n} \\ x_{2,n} \\ x_{3,n} \\ x_{4,n} \\ x_{5,n} \\ x_{6,n} \\ x_{7,n} \end{pmatrix},$$

the j-th coordinate of which is the size of the j-th stage in year n. We can then write our system as

(2.1.2) $$X_{n+1} = AX_n,$$

where the 7×7 matrix A hides all of the messiness of the system:

$$A = \begin{pmatrix} 0 & 0 & 0 & 0 & 127 & 4 & 80 \\ 0.6747 & 0.7370 & 0 & 0 & 0 & 0 & 0 \\ 0 & 0.0486 & 0.6610 & 0 & 0 & 0 & 0 \\ 0 & 0 & 0.0147 & 0.6907 & 0 & 0 & 0 \\ 0 & 0 & 0 & 0.0518 & 0 & 0 & 0 \\ 0 & 0 & 0 & 0 & 0.8091 & 0 & 0 \\ 0 & 0 & 0 & 0 & 0 & 0.8091 & 0.8089 \end{pmatrix}$$

A more visual way of representing the same model is its **life cycle graph** (Figure 6). In this graph, the **nodes** correspond to the stages $1 - 7$ of the population; they are pictured as circled numbers 1 through 7. An arrow from a node i to a node j means that a non-zero proportion of stage i transitions to stage j (this includes the possibility $i = j$). I have also indicated the values of these proportions next to the arrows: with this additional data, the life cycle graph allows us to fully reconstruct the system (2.1.2).

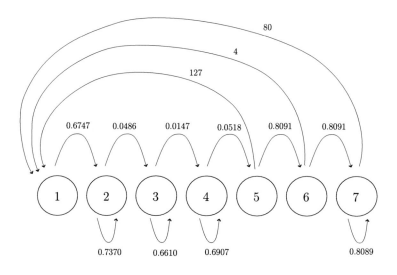

Figure 6. The life cycle graph of the turtle population

The system (2.1.2) is an example of a **first-order linear homogeneous system** of difference equations. It has a very simple form, each year, the vector describing the population is multiplied by A. So if X_0 is the initial data, then

(2.1.3) $$X_n = A^n X_0$$

But this simplicity is deceptive. As opposed to the n-th power of a single number, it is not at all clear what happens with A^n when n grows large. A natural question about the turtle population is whether it is endangered, that is, whether $A^n \to 0$ as $n \to \infty$, or on the contrary, the magnitude of the population grows, or at least remains stable. To analyze what happens with a matrix A when we raise it to a large power, we will need to dive into some Linear Algebra.

2.2. A feast for Linear Algebra fans

Let $A = (a_{ij})$ be an $m \times m$ square matrix. Let us begin by recalling that a non-zero column n-vector V is called an **eignevector** of A if

$$(2.2.1) \qquad\qquad AV = \lambda V$$

for some number λ, which is known as an **eigenvalue** of A. An equivalent way of writing (2.2.1) is

$$(2.2.2) \qquad\qquad (A - \lambda I)V = 0,$$

where I is the "unit" matrix with all ones on the diagonal, and zeros elsewhere, and 0 on the right-hand side stands for the zero n-vector. If we consider the coordinates of the vector V in (2.2.2) as unknowns, then what we have on our hands is a linear system of n equations with n unknowns. Moreover, this system evidently has a solution $V = 0$ no matter what the value of λ is. But we are looking for a non-zero solution. Recall, that the linear system (2.2.2) has more than one solution if and only if the determinant

$$(2.2.3) \qquad\qquad |A - \lambda I| = 0.$$

This is a polynomial equation in λ of degree n and it is known as the **characteristic equation**[1] of the matrix A. So, in principle, finding eigenvalues and eigenvectors is pretty straightforward. First, we set up the characteristic equation and find all of the eigenvalues λ_j, which are its roots. Then, for each eigenvalue λ we set up the system (2.2.2). It will have infinitely many non-zero solution vectors, each of which is an eigenvector with the same eigenvalue λ.

---

[1] Yes, a characteristic equation again. See §2.2.2.

All of this is something which is (or at least should be) familiar to you. Why is it useful for us? Let us first look at the special situation when all of the roots of the characteristic equation (2.2.3) are real and distinct. So we have n different real eigenvalues $\lambda_1, \ldots, \lambda_n$. Let us pick an eigenvector V_j for each λ_j. It is a well-known fact (see if you can prove it) that the vectors V_j are linearly independent. Let us change coordinates in the n-dimensional space by choosing these vectors V_j as the basis vectors. What will the matrix A look in the new coordinates? Well, it is not rocket science. Since $AV_j = \lambda_j V_j$, in the new basis our matrix takes the form

$$\hat{A} = \begin{pmatrix} \lambda_1 & 0 & 0 & \cdots & 0 \\ 0 & \lambda_2 & 0 & \cdots & 0 \\ 0 & 0 & \lambda_3 & \cdots & 0 \\ & & \cdots & & \\ 0 & 0 & 0 & \cdots & \lambda_m \end{pmatrix}$$

that is, it is a diagonal matrix whose diagonal terms are the eigenvalues. Choosing such a basis is known as **diagonalizing** the matrix A; we can write

(2.2.4) $$\hat{A} = C^{-1}AC,$$

where C is the "coordinate change" matrix, whose columns are the basis vectors V_j.

The beauty of this is that

$$\hat{A}^n = \begin{pmatrix} \lambda_1^n & 0 & 0 & \cdots & 0 \\ 0 & \lambda_2^n & 0 & \cdots & 0 \\ 0 & 0 & \lambda_3^n & \cdots & 0 \\ & & \cdots & & \\ 0 & 0 & 0 & \cdots & \lambda_m^n \end{pmatrix}$$

and it becomes very easy to say what happens to the matrix $\hat{A}^n$ (and, by extension, to the matrix $A^n = C\hat{A}^n C^{-1}$) when n grows large:

Theorem 2.2.1. *Suppose the matrix A is diagonalizable. If*

$$\max |\lambda_j| < 1,$$

then

$$A^n \xrightarrow[n \to \infty]{} 0.$$

The number $\max |\lambda_j|$ is known as the **spectral radius** of A, and we will denote it by $\rho(A)$. Furthermore, let us take any vector X_0 and write it out in the new basis:

(2.2.5) $$X_0 = c_1 V_1 + c_2 V_2 + \cdots + c_m V_m.$$

Then

(2.2.6) $$A^n X_0 = c_1 \lambda_1^n V_1 + c_2 \lambda_2^n V_2 + \cdots + c_m \lambda_m^n V_m.$$

Thus, we actually have a *formula* for the solution of the system $X_{n+1} = AX_n$:

$$X_n = A^n X_0$$

is given by (2.2.6).

In practice, this recipe could be quite cumbersome to use. In the model of a turtle population, for instance, the characteristic equation has degree 7 and even if we somehow succeed in finding the values of all λ_k's (and they all happen to be different) and V_k's, writing out X_0 as a linear combination of seven vectors will not be easy, and the formula will be difficult to apply. However, we can make the following simple and extremely useful observation.

Let us assume that $\rho(A)$ is attained on a single eigenvalue λ_j, that is, there exists a solution λ_j of the characteristic equation such that

$$|\lambda_j| > |\lambda_k| \text{ for all } k \neq j.$$

Such λ_j is called the **dominant eigenvalue** of A. Then assuming $c_j \neq 0$, when n is large, in the sum (2.2.6) the j-th term is going to dominate:

(2.2.7) $$A^n X_0 \approx c_j \lambda_j^n V_j.$$

Now, how is that important? Well, suppose, that we have a stage-structured population model, so different components of X_n correspond to the age groups. This, by the way, means that we should be able to pick V_j with non-negative terms (the expression on the left-hand side is non-negative, after all). Let $V_j = [v_1, v_2, \ldots, v_m]$ and let us **normalize** it by dividing each coordinate by the sum $v_1 + v_2 + \cdots + v_m$:

$$\tilde{V}_j = \left[\frac{v_1}{v_1 + v_2 + \cdots + v_m}, \frac{v_2}{v_1 + v_2 + \cdots + v_m}, \ldots, \frac{v_m}{v_1 + v_2 + \cdots + v_m} \right].$$

The normalized dominant eigenvector $\tilde{V}_j$ is, of course, still an eigenvector, and its terms sum up to 1. According to (2.2.7), it represents the *limiting distribution of age groups in our population model*:

> For a large n the fraction of the population corresponding to k-th stage is roughly the k-th coordinate of $\tilde{V}_j$.

To reach this conclusion, we had to assume that $c_j \neq 0$ in the decomposition (2.2.5). This is generally a safe assumption to make. Imagine, for simplicity, that

$$X_0 = \begin{pmatrix} x \\ y \end{pmatrix}$$

is two-dimensional, so there are only two coefficients c_1, c_2 in the formula (2.2.5). Let us say that c_1 corresponds to the dominant eigenvector V_1. The condition $c_1 = 0$ describes a straight line through the origin in the $x - y$ plane (can you explain why?). Suppose we were to pick X_0 at random. Think of throwing a dart at a dartboard with a vertical and a horizontal axes drawn, representing the coordinate plane. What are the chances that the dart would land precisely at the $c_1 = 0$ line? Nil! A *typical* point on the dartboard corresponds to $c_1 \neq 0$. Applying the same reasoning to higher-dimensional situation, we can say that for a typical vector X_0, the value of the coefficient $c_j \neq 0$.

So far, our considerations only applied to the case when the matrix A has m distinct eigenvalues. But what if this is not the case, and some of the solutions of the roots of the characteristic equation are repeated? It turns out that the conclusion of Theorem 2.2.1 still holds true in the general case[2]:

Theorem 2.2.1. *If $\rho(A) < 1$, then*

$$A^n \underset{n \to \infty}{\longrightarrow} 0.$$

Finally, the existence of a dominant eigenvalue is addressed by the following important theorem. Let us say that a life cycle graph is **strongly connected** if we can get from any node j to any other node k by following a sequence of arrows in the graph. For instance, the graph in Figure 6 is strongly connected since for every stage $s < 7$, there is an arrow leading to $s + 1$, and from stage 7 there is an arrow leading to stage 1 – and following this loop we can eventually visit any node, no matter where we start. A matrix A is called **irreducible** if its life cycle graph is strongly connected.

---

[2]See §2.2.1.

Perron-Frobenius Theorem. *Suppose that either (i) all terms in a square matrix A are positive, or (ii) all terms in A are non-negative and A is irreducible. In either case, there exists a dominant eigenvalue λ_j which is, moreover, a simple (that is, non-repeated) root of the characteristic equation. Moreover, the dominant eigenvalue is positive, and the corresponding eigenvector V_j can be chosen so that all of its coordinates are also positive.*

In this case, as before, the normalized dominant eigenvector $\tilde{V}_j$ represents the limiting relative size of the components of the vector $A^n X_0$ as $n \to \infty$, for a typical initial vector X_0.

2.2.1. Jordan normal form. An $m \times m$ matrix is diagonalizable if and only if there exist m linearly independent eigenvectors $V_1, \ldots, V_m$. A sufficient condition for this is that all of the eigenvalues are distinct. However, if some of the roots of the characteristic equation

$$|A - \lambda I| = 0$$

are repeated, there may not exist a basis of eigenvectors. But even in this case, there is a basis in which the matrix takes an "almost diagonal" form, known as the **Jordan normal form**. A matrix $\hat{A} = SAS^{-1}$ in the Jordan normal form still has the eigenvalues $\lambda_1, \lambda_2, \ldots$ on the diagonal. Each of the eigenvalues is repeated as many times, as its multiplicity as a root of the characteristic equation (so, in total, we still have m diagonal terms). In the case when an eigenvalue λ_j is repeated $r > 1$ times, we also put $r - 1$ ones on the off-diagonal, in each position which has a λ_j both to the left and below. So, for instance, if λ_j is repeated 3 times, we will have the following "block" in our matrix:

(2.2.8)
$$\begin{matrix} \lambda_j & 1 & \\ & \lambda_j & 1 \\ & & \lambda_j \end{matrix}$$

Thus, $\hat{A}$ can be written as a sum

$$\hat{A} = B + C,$$

where B is a diagonal matrix, and C is an upper-triangular matrix, whose only non-zero values are equal to 1 and lie on the off-diagonal. The fact that any matrix A can, by a change of basis, be brought into the Jordan normal form is known as the Jordan Decomposition Theorem after a French mathematician Camille Jordan. It is very useful in applications (but for some reason is rarely taught in a standard Linear Algebra course). For instance, armed with it, one is able to prove Theorem 2.2.1 in the case when A is not diagonalizable.

2.2.2. Note: turning equations into systems. It is not a coincidence that we use the same term "characteristic equation" both for difference equations (1.3.8) and for systems of equations (2.2.3) even when the two formulas look rather different. Given a difference equation of order k:

(2.2.9) $$x_{n+1} = a_{k-1}x_n + a_{k-2}x_{n-1} + \cdots a_0 x_{n-(k-1)},$$

we can easily turn it into an equivalent system as follows. Define new variables $y_{j,n}$ for $j = 1, \ldots, k$ by

$$y_{j,n} = x_{n-k+j}.$$

In this way, $x_{n-k+1} = y_{1,n}, x_{n-k+2} = y_{2,n}, \ldots, x_n = y_{k,n}$. We can then rewrite the single equation (2.2.9) as an equivalent system of k first-order equations:

(2.2.10) $$\begin{cases} y_{1,n+1} = y_{2,n} \\ y_{2,n+1} = y_{3,n} \\ y_{3,n+1} = y_{4,n} \\ \cdots \\ y_{k,n+1} = a_{k-1}y_{k,n} + a_{k-2}y_{k-1,n} + \cdots + a_0 y_{1,n} \end{cases}$$

which has the matrix

(2.2.11) $$A = \begin{pmatrix} 0 & 1 & 0 & \cdots & 0 \\ 0 & 0 & 1 & \cdots & 0 \\ & & \cdots & & \\ 0 & 0 & 0 & \cdots & 1 \\ a_0 & a_1 & a_2 & \cdots & a_{k-1} \end{pmatrix}$$

It is easy to see, in particular, that the system (2.2.10) and the equation (2.2.9) have the same characteristic equation.

It is usually possible to replace a system with an equation as well – we actually have already done it once with the generalized Fibonacci population (1.3.12) – but it is generally not worth the trouble.

2.2.3. Example: loggerhead turtles. Armed with this knowledge, we can now revisit the system (2.1.2). Since A is irreducible, Perron-Frobenius Theorem will apply to A. A computer algebra system finds the dominant eigenvalue to be equal to

$$\lambda \approx 0.94503.$$

This implies that the population is going extinct: the total number of turtles will converge to 0 as n increases. The normalized eigenvector

$$\tilde{V} \approx [0.20650, 0.66975, 0.11459, 0.00662, 0.00036, 0.00031, 0.00184],$$

corresponding to the dominant eigenvalue predicts the age group distribution for large values of n: you can see, for instance, that with time, small juveniles will constitute more than two thirds of the population.

2.3. A multi-billion dollar example

Okay, this example is not from Life Sciences, but I could not resist mentioning it. It is famous, and has produced an enormous wealth. I am talking about the Google PageRank algorithm, invented by the two founders of Google, Serge Brin and Larry Page when they were students at Stanford.

Before we discuss the algorithm itself, let us talk first about the principal difficulty of searching the Web. It is straightforward, and relatively inexpensive, to map out all of the Web and record the keywords appearing in each of the web pages in existence. Of course, such a record would need to be continuously updated, but at any given moment of time it would give a reasonably accurate snapshot of the information addressed by each of the pages. Now, suppose that we would like to use such a record to search for the key phrase "University of Toronto", for instance, because we are interested in learning more about the admissions process. Well, there are probably tens of thousands of web pages with this phrase, and our search will turn up *all* of them at once. Obviously, we will only be able to look at the first few pages that will appear on our screen, which are a small fraction of the overall number. We would expect that those first few pages are the most important search results somehow. And therein lies the problem:

How is the search engine to decide which of the pages with the given key words to display first, as the most important search results?

A naïve approach, such as counting the number of times the words "University of Toronto" appear on the page can easily go wrong. Suppose, for instance, that I own a fitness apparel store in Toronto and would like to market some of my wares to students. It would be laughably easy for me to add the keywords "University of Toronto" a few hundred times somewhere at the bottom of my store's web page to make sure it comes up on top of such a naïve search. This sort of thing would happen all the time with web searches pre-Google.

The approach of Brin and Page was based on a mathematical model for surfing the web. To begin describing it, let us start by labeling all of the web pages somehow, for instance, by assigning them numbers from 1 to N – here N is the total number of web pages in existence, and is, therefore *very* large. Let us populate the internet with web surfers (all of the humans with internet access), and let $x_{j,n}$ correspond to the the number of surfers visiting the j-th page at the n-th moment of time. To simplify things, let us assume that each person will spend precisely one minute on every web page they reach, no more, no less, and at the end of each minute will click on one of the links on that page. Again, for simplicity, let us assume that all links are equally likely to be clicked. So, if the j-th page contains k links, then, after accessing that page, exactly $1/k$-th of the surfers will follow each of those links.

Sounds simple enough, right? Of course, realistically, very few links lead to each idividual page. If we want to know what the surfer population of the j-th page will be at the moment of time $n + 1$ (minutes), we should look at every page m which links to it, count the surfers on that page at time n (that would be $x_{m,n}$), and multiply by the proportion of the links to page j from page m out of all the links embedded in page m (this way we will know what proportion of the surfers $x_{m,n}$ will end up on page j). Add these numbers up, and you get $x_{j,n+1}$:

$$x_{j,n+1} = \sum_{\text{all pages } m \text{ which link to page } j} \frac{\text{number of links from page } m \text{ to page } j}{\text{total number of links on page } m} x_{m,n}.$$

Let us see how this would work on an example of an internet with only four web pages pictured in Figure 7:

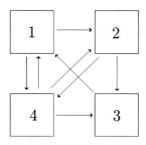

Figure 7. Web with only four web pages. The arrows represent the links.

For instance, the first web page has two web pages pointing towards it: the third and the fourth. There is, in fact, only one link embedded in the third web page, so every surfer starting there will inevitably go to page one at the end of the minute. But page four has three outward links, so only one third of $x_{4,n}$ will follow to page one at the end of the n-th minute. Applying this to every one of the pages, we end up with the following system of equations:

(2.3.1)
$$\begin{cases} x_{1,n+1} = x_{3,n} + \frac{1}{3}x_{4,n} \\[2mm] x_{2,n+1} = \frac{1}{2}x_{1,n} + \frac{1}{3}x_{4,n} \\[2mm] x_{3,n+1} = \frac{1}{2}x_{2,n} + \frac{1}{3}x_{4,n} \\[2mm] x_{4,n+1} = \frac{1}{2}x_{1,n} + \frac{1}{2}x_{2,n} \end{cases}$$

Hopefully, you have recognized by now a stage-structured population problem in disguise. The mathematics is exactly the same! We can abbreviate the system (2.3.1) if we gather the web-surfing human population into a column vector

$$X_n = \begin{pmatrix} x_{1,n} \\ x_{2,n} \\ x_{3,n} \\ x_{4,n} \end{pmatrix},$$

whose coordinates record the number of surfers visiting the j-th page during the n-th minute, and let the 4×4 matrix

$$A = \begin{pmatrix} 0 & 0 & 1 & \frac{1}{3} \\[2mm] \frac{1}{2} & 0 & 0 & \frac{1}{3} \\[2mm] 0 & \frac{1}{2} & 0 & \frac{1}{3} \\[2mm] \frac{1}{2} & \frac{1}{2} & 0 & 0 \end{pmatrix},$$

then the system (2.3.1) becomes:

(2.3.2)
$$X_{n+1} = AX_n.$$

The directed graph in Figure 7 is nothing but the life cycle graph of the matrix A. It is strongly connected, and thus, by Perron-Frobenius Theorem, the matrix A has a dominant eigenvalue. A computer agebra system can be used to find its value:

$$\lambda = 1$$

(there is some Linear Algebra magic which ensures that in our model the dominant eigenvalue is always equal to 1, but this is not going to be essential). The normalized dominant eigenvector is

$$\tilde{V} = \begin{pmatrix} \frac{10}{34} \\ \frac{8}{34} \\ \frac{7}{34} \\ \frac{9}{34} \end{pmatrix} \approx \begin{pmatrix} 0.294 \\ 0.235 \\ 0.206 \\ 0.265 \end{pmatrix}.$$

This means, that for large values of n, more than 29% of all surfers will find themselves on page 1, followed by more than 26% on page 4, more than 23% on page 2, and 20% and a bit on page 3. Logically then, page 1 is the most important one – as it gets the most visits, followed by pages 4, 2, 3.

This method of determining the relative importance of a web page does need some tweaking before being applied to the whole internet. If

$$X_n = [x_{j,n}]_{j=1,\ldots,N}$$

is the column N-vector in which the j-th entry stands for the number of surfers on the j-th page at the n-th minute, and $A = (a_{j,m})$ is the $N \times N$ matrix in which the entry $a_{m,j}$ represents the fraction of the links from page m which lead to page j, then most entries in the matrix A are zeros: there is a huge number of pages overall, and not that many links on each individual page. So, in particular, there is no reason for the life cycle graph of the whole internet in this model to be strongly connected. That would mean that Perron-Frobenius Theorem may not apply. So let us modify the model a bit. At the n-th minute some fixed (and probably small) proportion p of the surfers get bored with following the links, and will jump to any random page on the Web that happens to attract their interest. That will create an arrow from each page to each other page (including itself), and will make every entry of the matrix of the internet positive.

Mathematically, each non-zero entry in the matrix A will be multiplied by $(1 - p)$, as that is the fraction of the surfers which will continue following the links, and then each entry (zeros and non-zeros alike) will be incremented by $1/(Np)$ to reflect that $1/p$-th of the web surfing public will transfer to one of the N web pages selected at random.

To see how that would work in our example with four web pages, let us assume that $p = 1/5$-th of all surfers stop following the links and choose the next page at random. So, say starting from page one, $1/20$-th of the surfers would "teleport" back to page one, another $1/20$-th would go to page three, $4/10$-th would follow the link to page two and another $1/20$-th would teleport there (so in total $a_{2,1} = 9/20$), and in the same way $9/20$-th would end up going to page 4. The new matrix[3] will be

$$B = \begin{pmatrix} \frac{1}{20} & \frac{1}{20} & \frac{17}{20} & \frac{19}{60} \\ \frac{9}{20} & \frac{1}{20} & \frac{1}{20} & \frac{19}{60} \\ \frac{1}{20} & \frac{9}{20} & \frac{1}{20} & \frac{19}{60} \\ \frac{9}{20} & \frac{9}{20} & \frac{1}{20} & \frac{1}{20} \end{pmatrix}$$

The dominant eigenvalue is still $\lambda = 1$, the normalized dominant eigenvector is

$$\tilde{V} \approx \begin{pmatrix} 0.290 \\ 0.236 \\ 0.214 \\ 0.260 \end{pmatrix},$$

which is not much different, of course, from what we originally saw in this example. The ranking of the pages in the order of importance is still the same: $1, 4, 2, 3$.

And this is the original PageRank algorithm, which has revolutionized searching the Web.

2.4. Leslie models (or age-structured models)

Let us finish with a particular, and simpler, example of stage-structured models. Suppose, we divide the population into age groups corresponding to age intervals of the same length. For instance, demographers usually divide human populations into 5-year long stages (look at an image of the "population pyramid" of Canada illustrating such a division in Figure 8).

---

[3]In practice, this is a bit too elaborate. Things can be simplified by simply adding the same small value ϵ to every entry of the matrix A. This will have the same effect, the only difference is that the dominant eigenvalue would no longer be equal to 1.

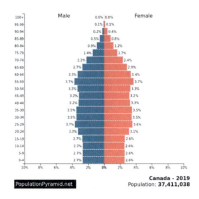

Figure 8. The population pyramid of Canada in 2019. Source: PopulationPyramid.net

The matrix for such a model[4] will look particularly simple. If s_j is the survival rate of the j-th age group, and b_j is the birth rate of the j-th group, and if we measure the time in the increments equal to the length of each stage, then the matrix will have the form

(2.4.1)
$$A = \begin{pmatrix} b_1 & b_2 & b_3 & b_4 & \cdots & b_{m-1} & b_m \\ s_1 & 0 & 0 & 0 & \cdots & 0 & 0 \\ 0 & s_2 & 0 & 0 & \cdots & 0 & 0 \\ 0 & 0 & s_2 & 0 & \cdots & 0 & 0 \\ 0 & 0 & 0 & s_3 & \cdots & 0 & 0 \\ & & & \cdots & & & \\ 0 & 0 & 0 & 0 & \cdots & s_{m-1} & 0 \end{pmatrix}$$

Such models are known as **age-structured,** or **Leslie** models (in honor of Patrick Holt Leslie who was one of the pioneers of using matrix models in population studies), and a matrix of form (2.4.1) is called a **Leslie matrix**.

Despite having simpler matrices, the division of a population into age groups of the same length is not always natural and not always practical. For instance, to replace the stage-structured model with a Leslie model in our first example, the population of loggerhead turtles would have to be

---

[4]Again, we are only modeling the growth of the female portion of the population

divided into 54 age groups of length of one year – leading to a 54×54 Leslie matrix.

2.4.1. An example of a Leslie model: sheep in New Zealand. Sheep farming is a major industry in New Zealand – apparently, at present writing, the country has 6 times more sheep than people. Here is a table for the annual birth/survival rates for female sheep in New Zealand taken from [Ca67]:

Age in years	Birth Rate	Survival Rate
0-1	0.000	0.845
1-2	0.045	0.975
2-3	0.391	0.965
3-4	0.472	0.950
4-5	0.484	0.926
5-6	0.546	0.895
6-7	0.543	0.850
7-8	0.502	0.786
8-9	0.468	0.691
9-10	0.459	0.561
10-11	0.433	0.370
11-12	0.421	0.000

This population is naturally described by a Leslie model with the 12×12 matrix

$$A = \begin{bmatrix}
0 & 0.045 & 0.391 & 0.472 & 0.484 & 0.546 & 0.543 & 0.502 & 0.468 & 0.459 & 0.433 & 0.421 \\
0.845 & 0 & 0 & 0 & 0 & 0 & 0 & 0 & 0 & 0 & 0 & 0 \\
0 & 0.975 & 0 & 0 & 0 & 0 & 0 & 0 & 0 & 0 & 0 & 0 \\
0 & 0 & 0.965 & 0 & 0 & 0 & 0 & 0 & 0 & 0 & 0 & 0 \\
0 & 0 & 0 & 0.950 & 0 & 0 & 0 & 0 & 0 & 0 & 0 & 0 \\
0 & 0 & 0 & 0 & 0.926 & 0 & 0 & 0 & 0 & 0 & 0 & 0 \\
0 & 0 & 0 & 0 & 0 & 0.895 & 0 & 0 & 0 & 0 & 0 & 0 \\
0 & 0 & 0 & 0 & 0 & 0 & 0.850 & 0 & 0 & 0 & 0 & 0 \\
0 & 0 & 0 & 0 & 0 & 0 & 0 & 0.786 & 0 & 0 & 0 & 0 \\
0 & 0 & 0 & 0 & 0 & 0 & 0 & 0 & 0.691 & 0 & 0 & 0 \\
0 & 0 & 0 & 0 & 0 & 0 & 0 & 0 & 0 & 0.561 & 0 & 0 \\
0 & 0 & 0 & 0 & 0 & 0 & 0 & 0 & 0 & 0 & 0.370 & 0
\end{bmatrix}$$

The Leslie matrix is irreducible (explain why) so Perron-Frobenius Theorem applies. The eigenvalue with the largest modulus is $\lambda \approx 1.1755 > 1$, so the population of sheep will continue to live long and prosper. The normalized eigenvector corresponding to λ is

$$V \approx [0.241, 0.173, 0.143, 0.118, 0.095, 0.075, 0.057, 0.041, 0.027, 0.016, 0.007, 0.002].$$

Its coordinates correspond to the proportion of the population each of the age groups will stabilize at over time.

2.5. Non-linear difference equations in population genetics

2.5.1. Why we will NOT study non-linear difference equations. Let me say something controversial: when it comes to non-linear equations, continuous-time models (differential equations) are vastly superior to discrete-time ones (difference equations). Consider the most basic example of a non-linear difference equation, in which the right-hand side is a *quadratic* function of x_n:

$$x_{n+1} = ax_n + bx_n^2.$$

There are literally hundreds of serious mathematical papers written on the behaviour of the sequence x_n for different choices of the coefficients a, b – it is that complicated. Equations of this sort are basic examples of so-called *chaotic dynamical systems*, which makes their study very important in understanding "Chaos", but at the same time makes them ill-suited for modeling.

By contrast, the non-linear continuous time model

$$\frac{dx(t)}{dt} = kx(t) + lx(t)^2$$

is dead easy to solve explicitly, and it is even easier to study the behaviour of the function $x(t)$. We will see this shortly in the following section of these notes. You have to go to 3-dimensional systems of differential equations to find examples of Chaos; one- and two-dimensional examples are very well behaved. [5]

There are some notable exceptions, however, when we are forced to consider dicrete-time models, since continuous-time approach simply would not make sense. Key examples of this in Biology come from population genetics. If we study how the genotypes of the offspring depend on the genotypes of the parents, then the passage of time is measured in generations, and is by necessity discrete. To get a taste of such models, let us describe one particularly fun example below. This discussion parallels the excellent exposition in [**EK05**].

2.5.2. Hardy-Weinberg law in population genetics. Even if you have never studied genetics in detail, you must have heard of its discovery by

---

[5]As a consolation of sorts, *linear* difference equations tend to be much more useful than their differential equation counterparts in modeling applications.

Gregor Mendel, a 19th century monk in what is now the Czech Republic. Mendel performed a series of experiments with pea plants. The best-known of these experiments had to do with the color of the flowers. Mendel artificially cross-pollinated purebred white flower and purple flower pea plants. In the resulting offspring plants the colors were not a blend. They were all purple. Mendel called the *biological trait* of having purple flowers *dominant*. He then took the experiment one step further, and cross-pollinated the purple-flowered offspring plants. In the "grandkids" generation Mendel again obtained both colors, but with a purple flower to white flower ratio of 3 : 1.

Let us give Mendel's explanation for this effect, using modern terminology. The *gene* for the color of the flowers in pea plants has two forms, known as *alleles*. The dominant allele corresponds to purple flowers, and we will use the capital letter A to denote it. The non-dominant, or *recessive* allele corresponds to white flowers and we will mark it with a. A plant has two copies of the gene, one from each of the parents. So purebred purple flowers will have two copies of A allele of the gene (we will simply write AA in this case), and purebred white flowers have aa.

When AA flowers are crossed with aa ones, all of the cross-pollinated offspring will be of a type Aa – getting one A from the purple parent and one a from the white one. Since A is dominant, they will all have purple flowers. What about the grandkids? Those are obtained by crossing Aa plants with Aa ones. All three combinations are now possible: AA, aa, and Aa. What are their relative frequencies? The first plant will contribute A in one-half of the cases. In one-half of that half, the second plant will contribute A, and in the other half of that half the second plant will contribute a. So 1/4 of the offspring will get A from the first parent and A from the second (type AA), and a further 1/4 will get A from the first parent and a from the second (type Aa). What if the first parent contributes a? Well, then we get a further 1/4 where the second parent contributes a (type aa), and 1/4 where the second parent contributes A (type aA which is the same as Aa – one dominant and one recessive allele).

		First parent	
		A	a
Second	A	AA	Aa
parent	a	Aa	aa

The end result? Half the grandkids are of type Aa, a quarter of type AA, and a quarter of type aa. In $3/4$ of them, A is present, so the flowers will be purple, and the remaining $1/4$ has two a alleles, and so will have white flowers. The ratio of purple to white will be exactly $3 : 1$!

The modern scientific understanding of genetic inheritance is, of course, much more sophisticated – but in what follows we will only need the basic Mendelian principles. Let us just metion in passing that the genetic material of complex organisms is carried in *chromosomes*, and *diploid* organisms have two pairs of them – one from each parent. There are many examples of dominant/recessive biological traits familiar to you, such as blue (recessive) or brown (dominant) eye color in humans, but they are usually functions of several genes rather than a single one.

Having discussed the basics, let us see how the frequency of dominant and recessive alleles of the same gene (with two alleles A and a) changes in a population from one generation to the next. To simplify things, let us assume that the size of the population does not change from one generation to the next, and is equal to N. Since each member of the population carries two copies of the gene, there are $2N$ copies of the gene in the population. Let us denote by p_n, q_n the frequencies of the alleles in the n-th generation:

$$p_n = \text{frequency of allele } A = \frac{\text{total number of alleles } A \text{ in } n\text{-th generation}}{2N},$$

$$q_n = \text{frequency of allele } a = \frac{\text{total number of alleles } a \text{ in } n\text{-th generation}}{2N}.$$

Naturally,

$$p_n + q_n = 1.$$

Let us assume that this particular gene does not affect the mating strategies or the survival (that is all of the combinations of the alleles have *equal evolutionary fitness*).

Let us denote:

- u_n = frequency of AA genotype in generation n;
- v_n = frequency of Aa genotype in generation n;
- w_n = frequency of aa genotype in generation n.

We then have:

(2.5.1) $$u_n + v_n + w_n = 1,$$

and

(2.5.2)
$$\begin{cases} p_n = u_n + 0.5v_n \\ q_n = 0.5v_n + w_n \end{cases}$$

Now let us see how the genotype frequencies will change from one generation to the next. First, let us see what are the frequencies of the genotypes of the mating pairs, by multiplying the frequency of the genotype of the "mother" by the frequency of the genotype of the "father":

		Mothers		
		u_n	v_n	w_n
	u_n	u_n^2	$u_n v_n$	$u_n w_n$
Fathers	v_n	$u_n v_n$	v_n^2	$v_n w_n$
	w_n	$u_n w_n$	$v_n w_n$	w_n^2

We can now use Mendelian principles to account for the genotypes of the offspring. A pair (AA, AA) will always produce an AA offspring. As we have seen, a pair of the type (Aa, Aa) will produce AA with frequency $1/4$, aa with frequency $1/4$, and Aa with frequency $1/2$. And so on. Summarizing for all of the possible scenarious we have:

		Offspring frequencies		
Parents	Frequency of parental genotype	AA	Aa	aa
(AA, AA)	u_n^2	u_n^2	0	0
(aa, aa)	w_n^2	0	0	w_n^2
(Aa, Aa)	v_n^2	$0.25v_n^2$	$0.5v_n^2$	$0.25v_n^2$
(AA, aa)	$2u_n w_n$	0	$2u_n w_n$	0
(AA, Aa)	$2u_n v_n$	$u_n v_n$	$u_n v_n$	0
(aa, Aa)	$2v_n w_n$	0	$v_n w_n$	$v_n w_n$

Summing up, we obtain the following system of equations:

(2.5.3)
$$\begin{cases} u_{n+1} = u_n^2 + 0.25v_n^2 + u_n v_n \\ v_{n+1} = 0.5v_n^2 + 2u_n w_n + u_n v_n + v_n w_n \\ w_{n+1} = w_n^2 + 0.25v_n^2 + v_n w_n \end{cases}$$

One last step: by (2.5.1) we can replace w_n with

$$w_n = 1 - u_n - v_n,$$

and the system (2.5.3) transforms into:

(2.5.4)
$$\begin{cases} u_{n+1} = u_n^2 + 0.25v_n^2 + u_n v_n \\ v_{n+1} = 0.5v_n^2 + 2u_n(1 - u_n - v_n) + u_n v_n + v_n(1 - u_n - v_n) \\ \quad = -0.5v_n^2 + 2u_n - 2u_n^2 - 2u_n v_n + v_n \end{cases}$$

Using (2.5.3) we find:

(2.5.5) $$p_{n+1} = u_{n+1} + 0.5v_{n+1} = u_n + 0.5v_n = p_n,$$

and thus

(2.5.6) $$q_{n+1} = 1 - p_{n+1} = 1 - p_n = q_n.$$

The equations (2.5.5) and (2.5.6) form the *Hardy-Weinberg* law of population genetics: **the frequencies of the two alleles of the gene in the population do not change from one generation to the next.** Think about it: this is quite counter-intutive. It would seem natural to assume that the recessive alleles would gradually vanish from the population – but the equations tell us otherwise. Of course, we have made many simplifying assumptions to derive this law, such as the fact that the two alleles have equal fitness, and the reality may be more complex.

It is a less-advertised fact that *after one generation*, the genotype frequencies u_n, v_n, w_n do not change either. If we look at the right-hand sides of the equations (2.5.4), and define the functions

$$f(u,v) = u^2 + 0.25v^2 + uv$$
$$g(u,v) = -0.5v^2 + 2u - 2u^2 - 2uv + v$$

so that $u_{n+1} = f(u_n, v_n)$, $v_{n+1} = g(u_n, v_n)$, then

$$f(f(u,v), g(u,v)) = f(u,v).$$

I would not recommend verifying this by hand, as the algebra is a bit tedious, but a computer algebra system would confirm this in an instant. This means that the frequencies do not change from one generation to the next, starting with the second generation. They do generally change from the initial generation to the following one (you can pick some random initial numbers u_1, v_1 – and it is very likely that u_2, v_2 given by (2.5.4) will turn out different), but increasing n will not lead to any further changes.

Sex-linked inheritance in fruit flies. In 1910, Thomas Hunt Morgan crossed red-eyed (wild-type) drosophila fruit flies and white-eyed mutants and made some key discoveries which led to the development of the chromososme theory of genetic inheritance.

It is now known, that the gene controlling the eye color belongs to the X sex chromosomes of the flies. The red allele is dominant. We will denote it by A, and will denote the recessive white allele by a.

The female (XX) flies have two alleles in three possible combinations: AA, Aa, aa; meanwhile, male (XY) drosophilas carry only one allele: "red" $A-$ or white $a-$. For simplicity, let us assume that male and female offspring appear with equal probability, and that drosophilas mate only once in their lifetime.

Sex linkage leads to interesting variations of Mendel's inheritance laws. For instance, if we cross wild-type red eyed females (AA) with white-eyed male mutants $(a-)$, then in the first generation all of the females will be of type Aa (getting one X chromosome with an A from the mother, and the other X chromosome with an a from the father), and all males will be of type $A-$ (getting X-linked A from the mother).

In the second generation, the mating table will look like this:

		Female	
		A	a
Male	A	AA	Aa
	$-$	$A-$	$a-$

Since A is dominant, AA, Aa, and $A-$ flies will have red eyes, and only $a-$ drosophilas will have white eyes, satisfying Mendel's $3:1$ proportions. However, if we look at males and females separately, then we see that the proportions are quite different, half of the second-generation males have white eyes, and none of the females do. See Figure 9 for an illustration.

It is a considerable hassle to check by hand whether or not Hardy-Weinberg law holds in this case, however, it is a useful *Maple* exercise. Let us denote:

- $x_{AA,n}$ = frequency of AA females in generation n,
- $x_{Aa,n}$ = frequency of Aa females in generation n,
- $x_{aa,n}$ = frequency of aa females in generation n,
- $y_{A,n}$ = frequency of $A-$ males in generation n,
- $y_{a,n}$ = frequency of $a-$ males in generation n.

It is not difficult to write down the difference equations describing the offspring. For instance, AA females in generation $n+1$ can be obtained by crossing AA females with $A-$ males or Aa females with $A-$ males of the n-th generation. In the first instance, AA females form half of the offspring (the other half are $A-$ males), and in the second instance, AA females form a quarter of the offspring. Let us express this, and all other possible outcomes as:

$$\begin{cases} v_{AA,n+1} = 0.5 x_{AA,n} y_{A,n} + 0.25 x_{Aa,n} y_{A,n} \\ v_{Aa,n+1} = 0.5 x_{AA,n} y_{a,n} + 0.25 x_{Aa,n} y_{A,n} + 0.25 x_{Aa,n} y_{a,n} + 0.5 x_{aa,n} y_{A,n} \\ v_{aa,n+1} = 0.25 x_{Aa,n} y_{a,n} + 0.5 x_{aa,n} y_{a,n} \\ w_{A,n+1} = 0.5 x_{AA,n} y_{A,n} + 0.5 x_{AA,n} y_{a,n} + 0.25 x_{Aa,n} y_{A,n} + 0.25 x_{Aa,n} y_{a,n} \\ w_{a,n+1} = 0.25 x_{Aa,n} y_{A,n} + 0.5 x_{Aa,n} y_{a,n} + 0.5 x_{aa,n} y_{A,n} + 0.5 x_{aa,n} y_{a,n} \end{cases}$$

I used v's and w's instead of x's and y's because there is a catch here: the v's and the w's do not add up to 1. To turn them into frequencies, we need to

Figure 9. The first and the second generations of offspring of a wild-type red-eyed female and a mutant white-eyed male. Source: *Wikimedia commons*

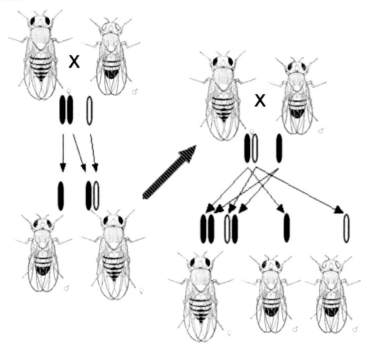

divide each of them by their sum:

$$S_{n+1} = v_{AA,n+1} + v_{Aa,n+1} + v_{aa,n+1} + w_{A,n+1} + w_{a,n+1}$$
$$= x_{AA,n}y_{A,n} + x_{AA,n}y_{a,n} + x_{Aa,n}y_{A,n} + x_{Aa,n}y_{a,n} + x_{aa,n}y_{A,n} + x_{aa,n}y_{a,n}.$$

The end result is:

$$
\left\{
\begin{aligned}
x_{AA,n+1} &= \frac{0.5x_{AA,n}y_{A,n} + 0.25x_{Aa,n}y_{A,n}}{x_{AA,n}y_{A,n} + x_{AA,n}y_{a,n} + x_{Aa,n}y_{A,n} + x_{Aa,n}y_{a,n} + x_{aa,n}y_{A,n} + x_{aa,n}y_{a,n}} \\[2ex]
x_{Aa,n+1} &= \frac{0.5x_{AA,n}y_{a,n} + 0.25x_{Aa,n}y_{A,n} + 0.25x_{Aa,n}y_{a,n} + 0.5x_{aa,n}y_{A,n}}{x_{AA,n}y_{A,n} + x_{AA,n}y_{a,n} + x_{Aa,n}y_{A,n} + x_{Aa,n}y_{a,n} + x_{aa,n}y_{A,n} + x_{aa,n}y_{a,n}} \\[2ex]
x_{aa,n+1} &= \frac{0.25x_{Aa,n}y_{a,n} + 0.5x_{aa,n}y_{a,n}}{x_{AA,n}y_{A,n} + x_{AA,n}y_{a,n} + x_{Aa,n}y_{A,n} + x_{Aa,n}y_{a,n} + x_{aa,n}y_{A,n} + x_{aa,n}y_{a,n}} \\[2ex]
y_{A,n+1} &= \frac{0.5x_{AA,n}y_{A,n} + 0.5x_{AA,n}y_{a,n} + 0.25x_{Aa,n}y_{A,n} + 0.25x_{Aa,n}y_{a,n}}{x_{AA,n}y_{A,n} + x_{AA,n}y_{a,n} + x_{Aa,n}y_{A,n} + x_{Aa,n}y_{a,n} + x_{aa,n}y_{A,n} + x_{aa,n}y_{a,n}} \\[2ex]
y_{a,n+1} &= \frac{0.25x_{Aa,n}y_{A,n} + 0.5x_{Aa,n}y_{a,n} + 0.5x_{aa,n}y_{A,n} + 0.5x_{aa,n}y_{a,n}}{x_{AA,n}y_{A,n} + x_{AA,n}y_{a,n} + x_{Aa,n}y_{A,n} + x_{Aa,n}y_{a,n} + x_{aa,n}y_{A,n} + x_{aa,n}y_{a,n}}
\end{aligned}
\right.
$$

I can do some *Maple* acrobatics and define a procedure **gen**(n) whose output is a list of five values $x_{AA,n}$, $x_{Aa,n}$, $x_{aa,n}$, $y_{A,n}$, $y_{a,n}$ recursively:

```
>gen:=proc(n)::list;
local vAA, vAa, vaa, wA, wa, S;
if n = 1
   then return inits;
   else
     vAA:=0.5*gen(n-1)[1]*gen(n-1)[4]+0.25*gen(n-1)[2]*gen(n-1)[4]:
     vAa:=0.5*gen(n-1)[1]*gen(n-1)[5]+0.25*gen(n-1)[2]*gen(n-1)[4]+
         0.25*gen(n-1)[2]*gen(n-1)[5]+0.5*gen(n-1)[3]*gen(n-1)[4]:
     vaa:=0.25*gen(n-1)[2]*gen(n-1)[5]+0.5*gen(n-1)[3]*gen(n-1)[5]:
     wA:=0.5*gen(n-1)[1]*gen(n-1)[4]+0.5*gen(n-1)[1]*gen(n-1)[5]+
         0.25*gen(n-1)[2]*gen(n-1)[4]+0.25*gen(n-1)[2]*gen(n-1)[5]:
     wa:=0.25*gen(n-1)[2]*gen(n-1)[4]0.25*gen(n-1)[2]*gen(n-1)[5]+
         0.5*gen(n-1)[3]*gen(n-1)[4]+0.5*gen(n-1)[3]*gen(n-1)[5]:
     S:=vAA+vAa+vaa+wA+wa:
     return([vAA/S, vAa/S, vaa/S, wA/S, wa/S]);
   end if;
end proc;
```

Here **inits** is a list of initial values. However, there is a high price to pay for the recursive definition of the procedure: *Maple* spends a loooong time evaluating it. It is much more efficient to use a **do** loop:

```
>gen:=array(1..5):gen:=[0.15,0.11,0.24,0.24,0.26]:
>L:=10:
>for n from 2 to L do
     vAA:=0.5*gen[1]*gen[4]+0.25*gen[2]*gen[4]:
     vAa:=0.5*gen[1]*gen[5]+0.25*gen[2]*gen[4]+
         0.25*gen[2]*gen[5]+0.5*gen[3]*gen[4]:
     vaa:=0.25*gen[2]*gen[5]+0.5*gen[3]*gen[5]:
     wA:=0.5*gen[1]*gen[4]+0.5*gen[1]*gen[5]+
         0.25*gen[2]*gen[4]+0.25*gen[2]*gen[5]:
     wa:=0.25*gen[2]*gen[4]+0.25*gen[2]*gen[5]+
         0.5*gen[3]*gen[4]+0.5*gen[3]*gen[5]:
     S:=vAA+vAa+vaa+wA+wa:
     gen:=[vAA/S,vAa/S,vaa/S,wA/S,wa/S]:
     print(gen);
  od:
```

My choice of the initial values of the frequencies was quite arbitrary – the only thing to worry about with them is that the first three values add up to 0.5 and so do the last two. When I run this code, I obtain the following results:

$$[0.09840000000, 0.2482000000, 0.1534000000, 0.2050000000, 0.2950000000]$$
$$[0.09122500000, 0.2450500000, 0.1637250000, 0.2225000000, 0.2775000000]$$

$$[0.09511875000, 0.2460125000, 0.1588687500, 0.2137500000, 0.2862500000]$$
$$[0.09324843748, 0.2453781250, 0.1613734375, 0.2181250000, 0.2818750000]$$
$$[0.09420273440, 0.2456570312, 0.1601402344, 0.2159375000, 0.2840625000]$$
$$[0.09373037108, 0.2455080078, 0.1607616211, 0.2170312500, 0.2829687500]$$
$$[0.09396774904, 0.2455801270, 0.1604521240, 0.2164843750, 0.2835156250]$$
$$[0.09384935916, 0.2455434693, 0.1606071716, 0.2167578126, 0.2832421875]$$
$$[0.09390862888, 0.2455616486, 0.1605297226, 0.2166210938, 0.2833789062]$$

Interestingly, the frequencies do not become constant, although, they do seem to converge. If we add another **print** command to the **do** loop, to see what happens with the frequency of the A allele:

```
print(gen[1]+0.5*gen[2]+0.5*gen[4]);
```

then we see that it remains unchanged at 0.325, which is a numerical evidence supporting Hardy-Weinberg law in this scenario.

**Exercises for
Chapter 2**

1. Let

$$A = \begin{pmatrix} 0 & 3 & 1 & 0 \\ 2 & 0 & 0 & 2 \\ 0 & 7 & 0 & 0 \\ 6 & 0 & 0 & 0 \end{pmatrix}$$

   Draw the life cycle graph for A and determine if A is irreducible.

2. Solve the following systems of difference equations written in matrix form

$$X_n = AX_{n-1},$$

   (a)

$$A = \begin{pmatrix} 1 & 2 \\ 3 & -4 \end{pmatrix}$$

   (b)

$$A = \begin{pmatrix} -1 & 1 & 2 \\ 0 & 3 & 1 \\ 0 & 0 & 1 \end{pmatrix}$$

3. For the square 3×3 matrix

$$A = \begin{pmatrix} \frac{1}{2} & \frac{1}{4} & 0 \\ \frac{1}{4} & \frac{1}{2} & \frac{1}{4} \\ 0 & \frac{1}{4} & \frac{1}{2} \end{pmatrix}$$

   verify that

$$A^n \xrightarrow[n \to \infty]{} 0.$$

4. Salmon is a fish that dies right after the birthing (spawning) process. A typical female salmon lays around 2000 eggs. Fertilized eggs hatch into *alevins* which are tiny embryo fishes with egg yolk sacs attached to their bodies. After they finish consuming all of the yolk, the small fishes emerge from the river bed and begin to swim around looking for food. At this stage of its life a salmon is called a *fry* (as in "a small fry"). Only about 10% of the eggs become fry. The tiny fishes are easy prey for various aquatic predators. After a year, about 10% of fry survive and grow into young salmon, known as *smolt*. Smolts leave the fresh water streams and migrate into the ocean, where they mature and reach

adulthood. It takes nearly two years for smolts to mature, with the survival rate of 70% a year.

Each Fall, 40% of the adults start an ardous migration to their natal streams. Half of them are spawning females, which lay eggs and die shortly thereafter, thus completing their life cycles. About 20% of the remaining adult salmon die each year, the rest survive until the following year.

(a) Construct a stage-structured model for a salmon population, starting with the fry stage. Assume that the population numbers for a given age remain nearly constant in consecutive years, to construct such a model.

(b) Will the salmon population described above grow or shrink with time?

(c) What is the ratio of fry to adults in an established salmon population?

5. **A very easy exercise.** Re-write the difference equation in a matrix form:

$$y_{n+4} = 67y_n + 4y_{n+1} + 55y_{n+3}$$

6. Consider a network with 6 web pages with the following link structure:

$$
\begin{array}{ccccc}
1 & \longrightarrow & 2 & \leftrightarrows & 3 \\
\uparrow & \searrow & \uparrow\downarrow & \searrow & \downarrow\uparrow \\
4 & \longleftarrow & 5 & \longrightarrow & 6
\end{array}
$$

(a) Write down the system of difference equations describing a random surfer of the network.

(b) Verify that the matrix of the system satisfies the Perron-Frobenius Theorem.

(c) Determine the Page Rank of each of the six pages.

7. Following [EK05], let us consider an annual plant which produces γ new seeds on average every Summer. The seeds can survive in the ground for up to two winters, and germinate in the Spring. The probability of a seed surviving each of the first two winters is σ. The proportion of one-year old seeds which germinate is α, and the proportion of two-year old seeds which germinate is β.

Construct a Leslie model for the seeds of the plant, and draw its life cycle graph.

8. 💡 **A fun but complicated example from population genetics.** Let us consider an example of a *lethal* recessive trait: the individuals with the genotype *aa* do not survive and leave no offspring. Again, denote p_n the frequency of the allele A, and q_n the frequency of the allele a in the n-th generation. Since there are no *aa*-type individuals, only two combinations of alleles are "allowed": AA and Aa. Let us denote u_n the frequency of the AA genotype in the n-th generation, and v_n the frequency of Aa. We then have

$$p_n + q_n = 1,$$

$$u_n + v_n = 1,$$

$$p_n = u_n + 0.5 v_n, \text{ and } q_n = 0.5 v_n.$$

(a) Find the system of difference equations expressing u_{n+1}, v_{n+1} in terms of u_n, v_n. There is a subtlety here – since not all of the combinations of alleles are allowed, the mating table will give two numbers which do not add up to 1, so you will need to divide by their sum to get u_{n+1}, v_{n+1}.

(b) Verify that

$$p_{n+1} = \frac{p_n}{p_n + p_n q_n} = \frac{p_n}{p_n (2 - p_n)}.$$

(c) Finally, verify that if $p_n < 1$, then

$$p_{n+1} > p_n.$$

This implies that

$$p_n \xrightarrow[n \to \infty]{} 1,$$

which means that the lethal allele will disappear from the population over time.

References for Chapter 2

[Ca67]   Caughley, G. *Parameters for Seasonally Breeding Populations*, Ecology **48**(1967) 834-839

[Cro87]   Crouse, D., Crowder, L., Caswell, H., *A Stage-Based Population Model for Loggerhead Sea Turtles and Implications for Conservation*, Ecology, **68**(1987), pp. 1412-1423.

[EK05]   Edelstein-Keshet, L., *Mathematical Models in Biology*, SIAM, 2005 (originally 1988).

First steps in non-linear modeling with differential equations

3.1. A brief introduction to differential equations

3.1.1. Definitions and first examples. A word of warning: I will often switch, as will be convenient, between the "prime" notation for the derivatives of a function (e.g. x'' for the second derivative, or $x^{(n)}$ for the $n-$th one) and the d/dt notation (e.g. $d^n x/dt^n$ for the $n-$th derivative).

The terminology used for continuous time models will sound very familiar. A *differential equation of order n* (or an *n−th order differential equation*) for an unknown function $x(t)$ is an expression of the form

$$(3.1.1) \qquad f\left(t, x(t), \frac{dx(t)}{dt}, \frac{d^2x(t)}{dt^2}, \ldots, \frac{d^nx(t)}{dt^n}\right) = 0,$$

or, in other words, any equation which involves the independent variable t, the function $x(t)$, and some of its derivatives, up to the $n-$th one. One example that we have seen already is the differential equation (1.2.3) of order 1 for radioactive decay:

$$P'(t) = -\lambda P(t)$$

for the unknown function $P(t)$.

All of our first examples of differential equations will be of order one, and will, moreover, have a simplified form:

(3.1.2) $x'(t) = f(t, x(t))$, or simply $x' = f(t, x)$.

An *initial value* for such an equation will be the value of the function $x(t_0) = x_0$ at some point $t = t_0$; an equation (3.1.2) together with an initial value form an *initial value problem*. An example of such a problem would be the compound interest equation $P' = rP$ together with the value of the principal $P(t_0)$ in the account on a certain date $t = t_0$. Intuitively, it is clear, that given such an information about the account, we (or the bank) should be able to calculate the value of the principal on any future date. But for a general equation of the form (3.1.2) it is far from obvious that a solution of an initial value problem should exist and be uniquely defined. For a discrete time model

$$x_{n+1} = g(n, x_n),$$

it is obvious that given an initial value x_0 we can uniquely reconstruct the whole solution sequence $x_1, x_2, x_3, \ldots$ as long as the right-hand side is *defined* for all values of n and x_n. But consider for instance the following initial value problem:

(3.1.3) $x' = \sqrt[3]{x}, \ x(0) = 0.$

Is there a unique solution? The answer, which happens to be a "no", is far from obvious. The following theorem gives some sufficient conditions for an initial value problem to have a unique solution:

> **Theorem 3.1.1 (Existence and uniqueness Theorem for first-order equations.).** *Suppose we are given an initial value problem*
> $$x'(t) = f(t, x(t)), \ x(t_0) = x_0.$$
> *Assume that there exists a rectangle given by the conditions $a < t < b, c < x < d$ in which both $f(t, x)$ and $\frac{\partial}{\partial x} f(t, x)$ are continuous; and let $t_0 \in (a, b), x_0 \in (c, d)$, so that our initial point lies inside the rectangle. Then there exists a unique solution $x(t)$ to the initial value problem. The function $x(t)$ is defined on some interval $t \in (a_1, b_1) \subset (a, b)$.*

Graphically, this means that we can fit a unique curve $x(t)$ through the point (t_0, x_0) in the plane, whose slope $x'(t)$ at every point $(t, x(t))$ satisfies the differential equation. Notice, that there is no guarantee that the function $x(t)$ will be defined for all values of t even if the right-hand side of the equation is defined (and "nice") for all (t, x). It is instructive to look at the following simple example:

(3.1.4) $$x' = x^2, \ x(0) = 1.$$

Existence and uniqueness of the solution are guaranteed by Theorem 3.1.1. You can, in fact, check that the solution is given by

$$x(t) = \frac{1}{1 - t}.$$

The interval around $t_0 = 0$ in which it is defined is not infinite ($x(1)$ is undefined), although the right-hand side of the equation is obviously "nice" for all values of (t, x).

We can visualize solving an equation (3.1.2) as follows. Let us superimpose a grid onto the $t - x$ coordinate plane, and at each point (t_*, x_*) of the grid draw a small vector with the slope $f(t_*, x_*)$ pointed left-to-right. Such a picture is known as a *slope field*. Solving the initial value problem given by $x(t_0) = x_0$ graphically means finding a curve which passes through the point (t_0, x_0) and "follows" the vectors of the slope field: that is, at each point of the plane it passes through, it is tangent to the vector of the slope field attached to this point.

Figure 10. On the left is the graph of the solution of the initial value problem (3.1.4). On the right you see that the initial value problem (3.1.3) does not have a unique solution: there are several possible ways to follow the slope field starting at the point $(0, 0)$.

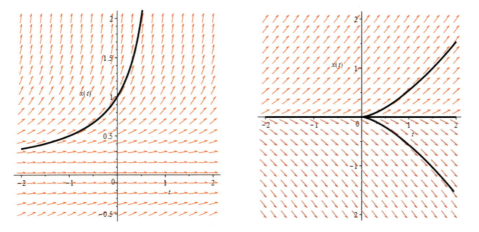

You can see two illustrations of this idea in Figure 10.

Will we always be able to find an explicit formula for the solution of an initial value problem, as the previous examples might suggest? Far from it. Even if x is absent from the right hand side of the equation, so it becomes an integration problem

$$x'(t) = f(t),$$

an explicit formula does not need to exist (you may have heard this before in your Calculus course). The existence of "nice" functions $f(t)$ for which the antiderivative $\int f(t)dt$ cannot be expressed explicitly as a combination of elementary functions was proven by Joseph Liouville in the 1830's. One prominent example is $\int e^{-t^2} dt$ which plays an important role in Statistics.

There are some very special classes of first order equations for which there is a procedure of finding a solution. We will only look at one such type of examples, known as **separable equations**. A separable equation, by definition, has the following form:

$$(3.1.5) \qquad \frac{dx}{dt} = g(t)h(x)$$

(as you will see, I wrote dx/dt instead of $x'(t)$ for a reason). By "separable" we mean here that all t's in the equation can be brought to one side, and all of the x's to the other (that is, separated). Yes, we are going to pretend that dx/dt is an algebraic expression in which the division sign stands for an actual division. Do not try this in a Calculus course!

If we do this, then we will get

$$(3.1.6) \qquad \frac{dx}{h(x)} = g(t)dt.$$

In for a penny, in for a pound – we might as well put integral signs on both sides, to pair with dx and dt. And, of course, each integral comes "plus a constant", of which we can keep only one:

$$(3.1.7) \qquad \int \frac{dx}{h(x)} = \int g(t)dt + C.$$

In outher words, if $W(x)$ is an antiderivative of $w(x) = \frac{1}{h(x)}$, and $G(t)$ is an antiderivative of t, then

$$(3.1.8) \qquad W(x) = G(t) + C.$$

There is an obvious issue with not always being able to find the formulas for $W(x)$ and $G(t)$, but setting that aside, the equation (3.1.8) is a straight-forward recipe for finding $x(t)$ – just solve for x. Since we have got to this step in such a creative fashion, let us verify that if $x(t)$ satisfies (3.1.8) then it is, in fact, a solution of (3.1.5). Indeed, we can differentiate both sides

$$(W(x(t)))' = (G(t))',$$

and use the Chain Rule on the left-hand side

$$W'(x(t)) \cdot x'(t) = G'(t), \text{ so } \frac{1}{h(x(t))} \cdot x'(t) = g(t),$$

which is what we needed. One word of caution: when we derived (3.1.7), we divided both sides by $h(x)$ which can never be done if $h(x(t)) \equiv 0$. So we should always check if $h(x(t)) \equiv 0$ is an extra solution to our equation, which we may have lost at that step.

Note that we get a one-parameter family of solutions, with C as a parameter. To nail down a specific function $x(t)$ we would need an initial value $x(t_0) = x_0$.

Let us see how this works on some examples.

3.1.2. Example 1. Let us start with the equation

(3.1.9)
$$\frac{dP}{dt} = rP,$$

which, if we set $r = -\lambda$, would become the equation of radioactive decay (1.2.3). Separating the variables, we have

$$\frac{dP}{P} = rdt.$$

We divided by $P(t)$, but $P(t) \equiv 0$ does satisfy the equation, so let us store it for later. Integrating

$$\int \frac{dP}{P} = \int rdt + C,$$

we get

$$\ln|P| = rt + C.$$

Exponentiating both sides, we obtain

$$|P| = e^{rt+C} = e^C e^{rt}.$$

Let us incorporate $\pm$ from $|P| = \pm P$ into a new constant $D = \pm e^C$, to get the solution
$$P = De^{rt}.$$
Note that the solution $P \equiv 0$ satisfies the same formula if $D = 0$, so we do not need to write it separately.

3.1.3. Example 2. Next, let us look at the example
$$\frac{dx}{dt} = x^2.$$
Then
$$\frac{dx}{x^2} = dt.$$
We lost a solution $x \equiv 0$ here, so let us again store it for later. Continuing,
$$\int \frac{dx}{x^2} = \int dt + C.$$
Thus,
$$-\frac{1}{x} = t + C \text{ or } x = -\frac{1}{t+C}.$$
This formula does not incorporate the solution $x \equiv 0$, which we will have to write separately. The final answer:
$$x = -\frac{1}{t+C} \text{ or } x \equiv 0.$$

3.1.4. Population modeling with first order differential equations. Suppose $x(t)$ is the size of a population at time t. As usual in Calculus, the derivative $x'(t)$ expresses the growth rate of the population. However, this is not what we typically mean by the "population growth rate" which is usually expressed in percentages, or fractions of the whole.

For instance, if you google the population growth rate of Canada in 2019, you will get back something like 1.4%, or 0.014. This expresses the proportion by which the population has grown in a year, and to find the actual rate of increase of the population, you will need to multiply this proportion by the size of the population. For Canada in 2019 you will get something like $531,000$ which is the actual annual growth rate for 2019. The quantity 0.014 is the *growth rate per capita*. In a general population model it has the form
$$\gamma = \frac{x'(t)}{x(t)}.$$

In the simplest scenario, γ could be a constant, independent both of the time and the present size of the population. Denoting this constant by r, we get the equation

$$r = \frac{x'(t)}{x(t)} \text{ or } x'(t) = rx(t).$$

This is our old friend, the equation (3.1.9). Its solution is the exponential function

$$x(t) = x_0 e^{rt}.$$

The exponential growth model has an obvious flaw. If $r > 0$, then

$$\lim_{t \to \infty} e^{rt} = \infty,$$

so the model predicts that the population will become arbitrarily large with time. This is, of course, not realistically possible given the finite amount of resources and space. There have to be constraints preventing the population from becoming too big. A natural way of expressing this is to make γ a decreasing function of x, so that when x becomes too large, the population will stop growing. In the simplest such model, γ is a linear function of x with a negative slope, conveniently written as:

$$\gamma = r(M - x),$$

where $r, M > 0$. The equation for the population growth then becomes

(3.1.10) $$x' = rx(M - x).$$

It is known as the **logistic differential equation**. Despite its simplicity, it is the most important population model – both in applications and as a thought inspiring example. One important feature of the equation is that the formula on the right-hand side has no dependence on t; the growth rate depends only on the size of the population itself. This is not always true, of course, in a realistic population. In most species the birth and death rates vary strongly with the season, for instance, so we would expect some periodic dependence of γ on t, with a period of 12 months. But this simplification will make the study of the solutions much easier.

Looking at the formula (3.1.10), we observe that if $x = M$ then the growth rate turns to zero. The function $x(t) \equiv M$ is a solution of the equation; which expresses the fact that the population would not change with time if its initial size is M. If $x(t)$ is less than M, then the growth rate is positive; if $x(t)$ overshoots M then the population rate is negative. Let us draw a little diagram, expressing this, see Figure 11. On the horizontal axis

Figure 11. A phase diagram for the logistic equation

$$x'(t)>0 \qquad\qquad x'(t)<0$$

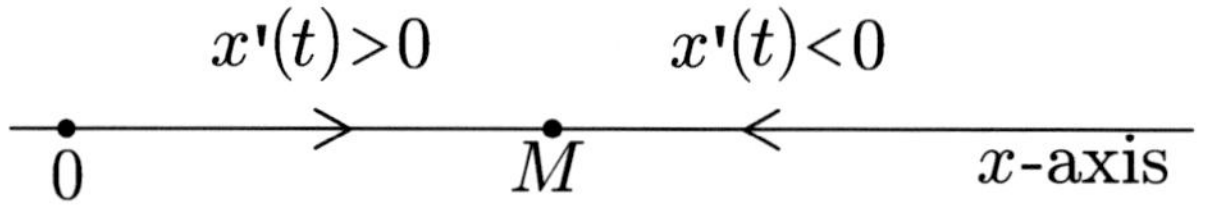

we will mark the value of the population $x(t)$. Since our equation has no t in it, the direction of movement along the x-axis will only depend on the initial point $x_0 = x(t_0)$ where we start. If $x_0 = 0$ then obviously $x(t) \equiv 0$ for $t > t_0$; and, as we have already discussed, if $x_0 = M$ then $x(t) \equiv M$ for $t > t_0$. If we start with $x_0 \in (0, M)$, then $x' > 0$, so x will increase with time. The population will move right along the axis as the arrow indicates, and will approach the limiting value M from the left. Similarly, if $x_0 > M$, then the derivative $x'(t)$ will be negative and the population will converge to M from the right. M is known as the **limiting population** and also as the **threshold population** (the threshold at which the growth changes sign).

Such a diagram is known as a **phase diagaram**. It captures all we need to know to make predictions about the future behaviour of the solution $x(t)$ given x_0. It is that simple! There is an obvious disadvantage to the diagram, it does not capture the exact values of $x(t)$. To get those, we would have to solve the separable equation (3.1.10). But it paints a clear qualitative picture.

3.2. Logistic model & Co.

3.2.1. Autonomous equations. Let us introduce some terminology: we will say that an equation

$$(3.2.1) \qquad\qquad x' = f(x)$$

is **autonomous**. A value c such that $f(c) = 0$ is called an **equilibrium point** of the equation, and if c is a equilibrium point, then $x(t) \equiv c$ is obviously a solution of the equation. Such a solution is called an **equilibrium solution**. Similarly to what we did for the logistic equation, we can plot a phase diagram for any autonomous equation. On the x-axis, we would mark the equilibrium points, they separate the intervals in which the sign of $x' = f(x)$ is constant, so the solution either increases ($f(x) > 0$) and we move right, or decreases ($f(x) < 0$) and we move left.

If arrows point *towards* an equilibrium solution from both sides, we call it **stable**. An example of a stable equilibrium is a limiting population $x = M$ in the logistic model. If our initial value x_0 deviates from the stable solution to either side, then the arrows in the diagram will bring it back towards the equilibrium. We can turn this into a formal definition:

Definition 3.2.1. An equilibrium solution $x(t) \equiv c$ of the equation (3.2.1) is stable if there exists $\delta > 0$ such that if the initial value $x_0 \in (c - \delta, c + \delta)$ then for the solution $x(t)$ we have

$$\lim_{t \to +\infty} x(t) = c.$$

If an equilibrium is not stable, we will call it **unstable**.

3.2.2. Solving the logistic equation. To fit the logistic model to real-life population data, we would need to go a step beyond the phase diagram and find a formula for the solution $x(t)$. The equation

$$\frac{dx}{dt} = rx(M - x)$$

is separable; separating the variables, we get

$$\frac{dx}{x(M - x)} = r\,dt, \text{ and } \int \frac{dx}{x(M - x)} = rt + C.$$

We have lost solutions $x \equiv 0$, $x \equiv M$, let us keep them in mind for the final answer. To integrate, we need to recall the partial fractions method, which gives

$$\frac{1}{x(M - x)} = \frac{1}{M}\left(\frac{1}{x} + \frac{1}{M - x}\right).$$

$$\int \frac{1}{M}\left(\frac{1}{x} + \frac{1}{M - x}\right) dx = \frac{1}{M}\ln\left|\frac{x}{M - x}\right|, \text{ so}$$

$$\ln\left|\frac{x}{M - x}\right| = Mrt + C.$$

Exponentiating both sides, we get

$$\left|\frac{x}{M - x}\right| = e^C e^{Mrt}.$$

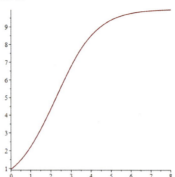

Figure 12. A solution of the logistic equation with $M = 10, r = 0.1$. The initial value $x(0) = 0.95$.

Let us again introduce a new constant $D = \pm e^C$, and write

$$\frac{x}{M-x} = De^{Mrt}, \text{ or } x = De^{Mrt}(M-x) = MDe^{Mrt} - De^{Mrt}x.$$

Solving for x, we obtain

$$x = \frac{MDe^{Mrt}}{De^{Mrt}+1}, \text{ or}$$

$$x = \frac{M}{1 + Ee^{-Mrt}},$$

where $E = 1/D$. We can recover the value of E from the initial value $x_0 = x(0)$. Substituting $t = 0$, gives

$$x_0 = \frac{M}{1+E} \text{ or } E = \frac{M-x_0}{x_0}.$$

We thus get

(3.2.2) $$x(t) = \frac{Mx_0}{x_0 + (M-x_0)e^{-Mrt}}.$$

Note that the one-parameter family of solutions given by the formula (3.2.2) does include the lost solutions $x \equiv M$ (when $x_0 = M$) and $x \equiv 0$ (when $x_0 = 0$).

It is instructive to look at a graph of a function of the form (3.2.2) with $x(0) < M$. Figure 12 is an example of such a graph. You can see that it looks very much like the graph of an exponential function when t is small, but then levels off for larger values of t at the limiting population level $x = M$.

In Figure 13 you can see examples of logistic curves fitted to real-life population data of harbor seals in Oregon, taken from [**Brown06**].

Figure 13. Figure taken from [**Brown06**].

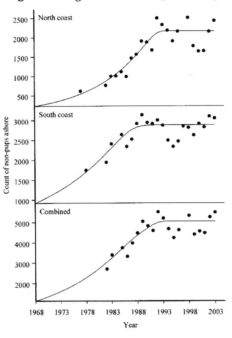

3.2.3. Harvesting a logistic population.

In our next example, qualitative analysis will be enough. Let us consider a farm, on which an animal population is grown and harvested. Assuming the population is described by a logistic model, this will lead to an equation of the form:

$$(3.2.3) \qquad x' = rx(M - x) - h,$$

where h is the *harvesting rate*. Our aim is to optimize the harvesting strategy to maximize the sustainable yield. There are two common strategies that we will consider. In the first one, h is proportional to the population size:

$$h = ex.$$

This is known as a *constant effort strategy*, where e represents the effort spent harvesting per member of the population. The second strategy is known as a *constant yield*, when

$$h = C,$$

is constant.

With the constant effort strategy we will get the equation

$$x' = rx(M - x) - ex, \text{ or}$$

$$x' = rx((M - e/r) - x).$$

This is again a logistic equation, in which the coefficients have changed. We should assume that $M > e/r$, which will ensure that the limiting population is positive. The sustainable yield is achieved when the population reaches its stable equilibrium $x = M - e/r$. Using the formula $h = ex$, we see that it is equal to

$$y(e) = e\left(M - \frac{e}{r}\right).$$

To maximize it we need to solve a Calculus problem. The function $y(e)$ is quadratic, its graph is a parabola pointing downwards, and it has a global maximum y_{max} when $y'(e) = 0$. This gives us $e = rM/2$, and

$$y_{max} = \frac{rM^2}{4}.$$

This is the maximal sustainable yield for the constant effort strategy.

Let us now consider the constant yield strategy. The equation becomes

$$x' = rx(M - x) - C.$$

The yield is constant, of course, $y = C$. What happens when we try to maximize it? Solving for the equilibrium points, we get a quadratic equation

$$-rx^2 + rMx - C = 0.$$

It has two solutions when $r^2M^2 - 4rC > 0$, or simply when

$$\textbf{(a) } C < \frac{rM^2}{4}.$$

There will only be one solution when

$$\textbf{(b) } C = \frac{rM^2}{4},$$

and no solutions if

$$\textbf{(c) } C > \frac{rM^2}{4}.$$

The three scenarios are depicted in Figure 14. We see that in case (c), the rate of harvesting exceeds the farms' capacity: the population will decline with time. In theory, $x(t)$ will converge to $-\infty$; in practice, it will simply decline to 0.

In cases (a) and (b) there are non-zero equilibrium points to arrest the population decline. So it would seem that the yield can be pushed all the way to

$$y = \frac{rM^2}{4},$$

which is the same value as we obtained for the constant effort strategy.

Figure 14. Phase diagram for the three possible scenarios for a logistic equation with a constant yield harvesting

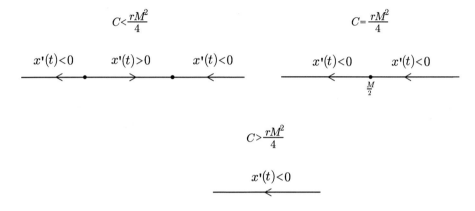

However, such a farm would not be sustainable in the long term. The equilibrium point in case (b) is not stable. In practice, this means that a small fluctuation in the size of the population which temporarily pushes it below this point would start an unstoppable decline. This means that to keep the farm sustainable in this scenario, the harvesting rate would have to be kept below the theoretically optimal value $rM^2/4$ (probably, well below it, to make sure that the farm will not be pushed to extinction by a small fluctuation in the population size).

In summary, if we are looking to optimize the sustainable yield, then the constant effort strategy is clearly preferable.

3.2.4. Solutions of autonomous equations: a theorem. Our approach to describing autonomous equations via phase portraits may seem a little *ad hoc*, but the following theorem shows that it is completely rigorous.

Theorem 3.2.1 (Properties of solutions of autonomous equations). *Consider an autonomous equation*

$$x' = f(x)$$

in which the right hand side is a differentiable function of x with a continuous derivative (so as to satisfy the conditions of the Existence and Uniqueness Theorem). Let x(t) be a solution. Then, the following are true:

(1) *either x(t) is an equilibrium solution (x(t) $\equiv$ x_0) or x(t) is a strictly monotone function of t (strictly increasing or strictly decreasing);*

(2) *either*

$$\lim_{t \to +\infty} x(t) = \infty, \text{ or } \lim_{t \to +\infty} x(t) = x_0,$$

where x_0 is an equilibrium point;

(3) *Similarly, either*

$$\lim_{t \to -\infty} x(t) = \infty, \text{ or } \lim_{t \to -\infty} x(t) = x_0,$$

where x_0 is an equilibrium point.

The theorem tells us that only two things can happen with a solution $x(t)$ of an autonomous equation as t grows large: it may either converge to an equilibrium solution or converge to infinity. Moreover, its dependence on t is monotone, so on the x-axis, the solution either always moves to the right, or always moves to the left, as t increases. This is why we were so successful in describing our models using phase portraits. Indeed, by putting down on the x-axis all of the equilibrium points of $x' = f(x)$, as well as the arrows to indicate the direction in which $x(t)$ changes with time, we can capture all of the essential features of the behaviour of $x(t)$.

The proof of the theorem is not difficult, but it is an actual proof, using some actual math. So if you are a fan of mathematical reasoning, enjoy, and if not, then steer clear.

Proof. To prove (1), assume that $x(t)$ is not strictly monotone, so there exist two distinct values $t_1 \neq t_2$ such that

$$x(t_1) = x(t_2).$$

By Rolle's Theorem, there exists $t_0 \in [t_1, t_2]$ such that $x'(t_0) = 0$. Set $x(t_0) = x_0$. Then

$$x'(t_0) = f(x_0) = 0,$$

so x_0 is an equilibrium point. Then $\hat{x}(t) \equiv x_0$ is an equilibrium solution. By the uniqueness part of the Existence and Uniqueness Theorem, any two solutions satisfying the same initial condition $x(t_0) = x_0$ must coincide. Hence,

$$x(t) = \hat{x}(t) \equiv x_0.$$

Let us now prove (2). Suppose that $x(t)$ is not an equilibrium solution, otherwise the proof would be trivial. By part (1), the function $x(t)$ is strictly monotone. Let us assume that $x(t)$ is strictly increasing (the proof in the case when $x(t)$ is decreasing is identical). If $x(t)$ is not bounded for $t > 0$, then for every $B \in \mathbb{R}$ there exists t_1 such that $x(t_1) > B$, and since $x(t)$ is increasing, we have $x(t) > B$ for all $t > t_1$. This is the definition of

$$\lim_{t \to +\infty} x(t) = +\infty.$$

In the case when $x(t)$ is bounded for $t > 0$, let x_0 be the strict upper bound of $x(t)$, that is, the smallest real number such that $x(t) \leq x_0$ for all $t > 0$[1].

First, note that for every $\epsilon > 0$, there exists t_1 such that $x(t_1) \in (x_0 - \epsilon, x_0]$. For if there were an $\epsilon_1 > 0$ such that $x(t)$ is *never* larger than $x_0 - \epsilon_1$, then $x_0 - \epsilon_1$ would also be an upper bound, which would contradict the choice of x_0. Since $x(t)$ is an increasing function, $x(t) \in (x_0 - \epsilon, x_0]$ for all $t \geq t_1$, which is the definition of

$$\lim_{t \to +\infty} x(t) = x_0.$$

Finally, let us show that $f(x_0) = 0$. Assume the contrary. Note that $f(x_0)$ cannot be negative – otherwise, $f(x) < 0$ for the nearby values of x, and $x(t)$ would not be an increasing function near x_0. Thus, necessarily, $f(x_0) > 0$. By continuity of $f(x)$, there exist $\epsilon > 0$ such that $f(x) > f(x_0)/2$ for all $x \in (x_0 - \epsilon, x_0]$. Let t_1 be such that $x(t) \in (x_0 - \epsilon, x_0]$ for all $t \geq t_1$. By the Fundamental Theorem of Calculus, for $t > t_1$ we have

$$x(t) = x(t_1) + \int_{t_1}^{t} x'(s)ds = x(t_1) + \int_{t_1}^{t} f(x(s))ds$$

$$> x(t_1) + \int_{t_1}^{t} \frac{f(x_0)}{2}ds > x(t_1) + (t - t_1)\frac{f(x_0)}{2}.$$

The expression on the right converges to $+\infty$ as $t \to +\infty$, which leads us to a contradiction.

Part (3) is proved in the same way as part (2), and will be left as an exercise. $\square$

3.3. An important non-autonomous example: Gompertz model

3.3.1. Gompertz law of human mortality. In 1825, a self-taught statistician Benjamin Gompertz formulated a remarkable in its simplicity law of human mortality [**Gom1825**]. To state it, let us recall that the *mortality rate in a population* is measured as the proportion of the population dying per

---

[1]The mathematical term for a strict upper bound is the *supremum*, and the notation is $x_0 = \sup\{x(t)\ t > 0\}$.

unit of time. Statisticians and actuaries are typically concerned with the mortality rate $m(n)$ of the population of a given age of n years, which will be calculated as

$$(3.3.1) \qquad m(n) = \frac{\text{number of deaths of people aged } n \text{ years}}{\text{number of all people aged } n \text{ years}}$$

Being more formal, let us denote $L(t)$ the size of the population of age t (again be measured in years). If Δt is an increment of time, then the corresponding *mortality rate at age t per time* Δt is given by

$$(3.3.2) \qquad -\frac{\Delta L(t)}{L(t)\Delta t}$$

Here $\Delta L(t)$ is the change in the size of the population aged t years due to deaths over the interval of time Δt (since we are only looking at the mortality rate, we are not looking at any other causes of change: births, migration, etc). The minus sign is in front of the expression (3.3.2) since the change $\Delta L(t)$ is obviously negative.

The standard procedure in Calculus is to pass to the limit as $\Delta t \longrightarrow 0$, to obtain the *instantaneous mortality rate at time t*:

$$(3.3.3) \qquad \mu(t) = \lim_{\Delta t \to 0} -\frac{\Delta L(t)}{L(t)\Delta t} = -\frac{L'(t)}{L(t)}.$$

In reality, the rate per unit of time does not change very much in a year (unless we are talking about the very first few years of life), so for integer values of t (and setting $\Delta t = 1$) we will have

$$\mu(t) \approx m(t);$$

and statisticians use the two quantities interchengeably. It is worth noting, that, by the Chain Rule,

$$(3.3.4) \qquad \mu(t) = -\frac{L'(t)}{L(t)} = -\frac{d}{dt}\log(L(t)).$$

Evidently, for the adult population, we expect the mortality rate $\mu(t)$ to increase with age. The empirical law discovered by Gompertz is that $\mu(t)$ is an *exponential* function of t:

$$(3.3.5) \qquad \mu(t) = r\exp(at), \quad r, a > 0.$$

An equivalent way of formulating the law is that the natural logarithm of the death rate $\log(\mu(t))$ is a linear function of the age t:

$$\log\mu(t) = at + b,$$

where $b = \log r$.

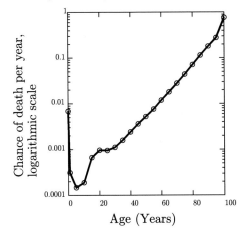

Figure 15. Estimated annual mortality rate $m(t)$ at each age t years, for the U.S. in 2003 (source: CDC). Note that the vertical scale is *logarithmic*. The dots fit beautifully to a straight line after about age 30.

Gompertz law is in a remarkably good agreement with the data for adults (from about age 30 to age 80 in North America at present time), as can be seen in Figure 15. It is widely used to calculate the value of life insurance in acturial science. Empirically, the slope $a \approx 0.085$. As with any exponential growth, it is instructive to calculate the doubling time of the death rate, given by

$$\exp(at) = 2, \text{ or } t = \log 2/a \approx 8 \text{ years.}$$

So every 8 years the risk of dying roughly doubles. Most life insurance quotes are given in 10-year increments, and playing with an online calculator for a large Canadian insurance company I found, for example, the monthly premium for a \$ 500,000 policy to be equal to \$ 80 for a male aged 40-44, and 197.50 for a male aged 50-54. The ratio of 2.4 is a good approximation for $\exp(10 \cdot 0.085) \approx 2.34$.

If we subscribe to the Gompertz model of mortality then the number $L(t)$ of people of age t alive satisfies the differential equation

(3.3.6) $$L'(t) = -r \exp(at) L(t).$$

This is a separable equation, which can be solved without difficulty (do it as an exercise!). The solution has the form

(3.3.7)
$$L(t) = C \exp\left(-\frac{r}{a}\exp(at)\right),$$

substituting $t = 0$ gives $L_0 = L(0) = C\exp(-\frac{r}{a})$, so that

(3.3.8)
$$L(t) = L_0 \exp\left(\frac{r}{a}(1 - \exp(at))\right).$$

Increasing life expectancy changes the constant r in Gompertz law. Empirically, at present $r \approx 0.0002$ [**FP96**]. Since $a \approx 0.085$, the equation (3.3.8) translates into

$$L(t) \approx L_0 \exp(0.0023(1 - \exp(0.085t))).$$

To get a sense of the limitations this puts on the life expectancy, let us plug in $t = 100$ (the Gompertz Law does not quite work for ages this high, but we are just doing a "back of an envelope" calculation here), to get $L(100) \approx L_0 \times 10^{-5}$, and we should think of 10^{-5} here as the *probability of surviving to age* 100 for people born 100 years ago. It is quite low indeed. Plugging in $t = 150$ we get the probability of survival equal to 7×10^{-345} which is prohibitively small (and which is why nobody has reached the age of 150).

The Gompertz law is a remarkable, seemingly universal, law of nature, that works across different species. What are the reasons for such a simple mathematical formula governing the rules of life and death? Let me bring to your attention a delightfully short (and nicely written) paper [**Shkl05**] in which a very simple explanation is given. I do not wish to tell you that this is indeed the "correct" explanation, but rather to illustrate how such an explanation may be designed in terms of our understanding of the way in which our bodies function. I will paraphrase it below as follows.

Let us adopt a very simplistic view of the workings of the immune system. Suppose a population of "defective" cells (cancer cells, cells that produce defective proteins, mutated cells which do not fullfil their normal functions, etc) becomes fatal if the organism's defences give it time τ to grow to a critical size. If these bad cells encounter an immune response before time τ has elapsed, then they will be destroyed and the danger to life will be averted. We can imagine the agents of the immune system as "cops" which patrol the body, looking for "robbers" – i.e. the defective cells. Let us assume that the cops patrol randomly, and for a healthy t-year old adult, the average number of encounters of a cell with a cop in time τ is some large number $N = N(t)$. What are the chances of a robber eluding a cop long enough to grow to a critical size and cause death?

To simplify the problem a bit, let us divide the time interval of length τ into $k > N$ equal subintervals of length τ/k for some large k, and assume that the chance of encountering a cop in each one of them is N/k (which, of course, works out to $k \cdot \frac{N}{k} = N$ encounters on average over time τ). What is the probability of *not* encountering a cop in an interval of length τ/k? It is $1 - N/k$. Since there are k such intervals, and the encounters happen independently of each other, the probability of not seeing a cop even once in time τ is

$$(3.3.9) \qquad \left(1 - \frac{N}{k}\right)^k.$$

Recall from Calculus, that

$$(3.3.10) \qquad \lim_{k \to \infty} \left(1 - \frac{N}{k}\right)^k = \exp(-N),$$

which is the probability of a robber never encountering a cop in time τ, without our simplifying assumption.

It is worth noting that the probability of encountering a cop M times is given by the *Poisson distribution*

$$P(M) = \frac{N^M \exp(-N)}{M!};$$

our calculation was for the particular case $M = 0$ (can you derive this formula for an arbitrary M using the same line of reasoning?).

It is natural to assume that the effectiveness of the immune system decreases with age, so $N(t)$ is a decreasing function of t. The simplest formula for a decreasing function is linear, with

$$N(t) = -at - b \text{ where } a > 0.$$

Substituting this into (3.3.10), we get the following formula for the probabilty of dying at age t:

$$\mu(t) = \exp(at + b),$$

which is the Gompertz law!

Gompertz model has found many other applications in biology, in particular, in cancer research. It turns out that the growth rate of solid tumors *per unit of volume* decreases exponentially with time. This gives the formula

$$(3.3.11) \qquad \frac{V'(t)}{V(t)} = r \exp(-mt),$$

where $V(t)$ is the volume of the tumor at time t. This is nothing other than Gompertz law (3.3.5) with a *negative* value of $a = -m$. We can rewrite it using the Chain Rule formula

$$\frac{d}{dt} \log V(t) = \frac{V'(t)}{V(t)}$$

as

(3.3.12) $\dfrac{d}{dt}\log V(t) = r\exp(-mt)$ or $\log\dfrac{d}{dt}\log V(t) = \log r - mt$.

The solution is

(3.3.13) $V(t) = V_0 \exp\left(\dfrac{r}{m}(1 - \exp(-mt))\right).$

The nice thing about this formula is that it makes biological sense ($V(t) > 0$) for all values of t. The graph of the function $V(t)$ with completely arbitrarily chosen values $V_0 = 10$, $r = 1$, $m = 0.5$ is given in Figure 16.

Figure 16. A graph of a Gompertz function $V(t)$ describing the volume of a solid tumor at time t.

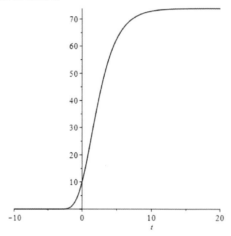

Observe, that Gompertz growth with negative a looks very similar to logistic growth; the graph has horizontal asymptotes

$$V(t) \underset{t\to+\infty}{=} V_0 \exp\left(\dfrac{r}{m}\right), \text{ and } V(t) \underset{t\to-\infty}{=} 0.$$

For $t \approx 0$, replacing $\exp(-mt)$ with its first-order Taylor polynomial approximation $1 - mt$, we find

$$V(t) \approx V_0\exp(rt) \text{ when } t \text{ is small.}$$

On the other hand, using the first-order Taylor approximation $\exp(a + x) \approx \exp(a) + \exp(a)x$ when $x \approx 0$, we see that

$$V(t) \approx V_0\exp\left(\dfrac{r}{m}\right)\left(1 - \dfrac{r}{m}\exp(-mt)\right) \text{ when } t \to +\infty.$$

Thus, a Gompertz growth is a combination of two exponential regimes: it starts with a nearly exponential growth while $V(t)$ is small, and then "levels off" at $V_0 \exp(r/m)$ exponentially fast when t is large.

**Exercises for
Chapter 3**

1. Newton's law of cooling (which should have been named more accurately "Newton's law of change of temperature", since it applies to both cooling and heating) says that the rate of change of temperature of an object is proportional to the difference between the temperature of the object and the temperature of the environment.

    (a) Assume that the temperature of the environment is constant, and write down a differential equation expressing this law. Pay attention to the sign of the coefficient of proportionality.

    (b) Find the general solution of the equation.

    (c) Draw a phase diagram to describe how the temperature of an object changes with time.

2. **Bor-r-ring... let's practice solving separable equations.** Find the general solution for each of the following:

    (a)
    $$y' = y^2 x$$

    (b)
    $$\frac{dy}{dx} = 3x^2 e^{-2y}$$

    (c)
    $$\frac{dy}{dx} = \frac{xy}{\sqrt{1 + x^2}}$$

3. Consider the initial value problem (3.1.3). Verify that it does not satisfy the conditions of the Existence and Uniqueness Theorem, and prove that it has more than one solution (as seen in Figure 10).

4. Consider the phase diagram in Figure 17. Write an autonomous differential equation which matches this diagram.

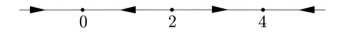

Figure 17. Phase diagram for Problem 3.

5. 💡 Prove that there does not exist an autonomous differential equation $x' = f(x)$ which has two stable equilibrium points at 0, 1 and no other equilibrium points.

6. Solve Gompertz equation (3.3.6) to verify the formula (3.3.7).

7. There are many examples of natural harvesting strategies of populations of prey by predators. One of them, in particular, has the form
$$h = \frac{ax}{1 + bx}.$$
In ecological literature this is known as *type II functional response* by the predators to the number x of prey. One example would be a pack of wolves, hunting a population of caribou. If the number of caribou x is small, then the harvesting rate $h \approx ax/b$ will be nearly proportional to the number of sightings of caribou (which is proportional to x). On the other hand, as the numbers of prey increase, the wolves no longer need to spend a significant time or effort hunting the food, and the hunting rate reaches a saturation: as x grows large, $h(x) \to a/b$ which is a constant.

    This strategy is thus a combination of the constant effort and constant yield strategies. Let us consider the logistic model with this type of harvesting term. To simplify the equation, let us set $b = r = 1$, so we get
$$x' = x(M - x) - \frac{ax}{1 + x}.$$
Let $a < M$. Investigate the phase diagram of the model to describe the long-term behaviour of $x(t)$. Note that you should only consider $x \geq 0$.

8. Use a computer algebra system to investigate a logistic population growth model in which the threshold M is not constant, but instead varies periodically with period P:
$$M = M_0(1 - \epsilon \sin(2\pi x/P)),$$
where ϵ is a small positive number. This could, for example, be a model for a population whose living conditions are affected by the change in seasons (in which case, $P = 12$ months).

References for Chapter 3

[Brown06]   R. Brown, B. Wright, S. Riemer, J. Laake. *Trends in abundance and current status of harbor seals in Oregon: 1977–2003*. Marine Mammal Science. **21**(2006), 657 - 670.

[Gom1825]   B. Gompertz, *On the Nature of the Function Expressive of the Law of Human Mortality, and on a New Mode of Determining the Value of Life Contingencies*. Philosophical Transactions of the Royal Society of London. **115**(1825), 513 585.

[FP96]   C. Finch, M. Pike. *Maximum Life Span Predictions From the Gompertz Mortality Model*, J. of Gerontology, **51A**(1996), B183-B194

[Shkl05]   B. Shklovskii, *A simple derivation of the Gompertz law of human mortality*, Theory in Biosciences, **123**(2005), 431-433.

Equilibrium points of non-linear systems (connecting the dots)

4.1. An essential tool: linear systems of differential equations

4.1.1. The basics. As we are going to see below, the mathematics of linear systems of differential equations will be *very* similar to what we have already seen with linear systems of difference equations. But I will still discuss them, and not because I want to waste your time: understanding linear systems will be our key for analyzing non-linear ones, which is where all of the fun is. So, without any further ado, let us make the necessary definitions.

A **linear system of differential equations of order** 1 has the form:

(4.1.1)
$$\begin{cases} x_1'(t) = a_{1,1}(t)x_1(t) + a_{1,2}(t)x_2(t) + \cdots + a_{1,n}(t)x_n(t) + b_1(t), \\ x_2'(t) = a_{2,1}(t)x_1(t) + a_{2,2}(t)x_2(t) + \cdots + a_{2,n}(t)x_n(t) + b_2(t), \\ \cdots \\ x_n'(t) = a_{n,1}(t)x_1(t) + a_{n,2}(t)x_2(t) + \cdots + a_{n,n}(t)x_n(t) + b_n(t). \end{cases}$$

Here, $x_1(t), \ldots, x_n(t)$ are the unknown functions. As with systems of difference equations, the notation becomes much neater in a matrix form:

(4.1.2)
$$X'(t) = A(t)X(t) + B(t).$$

Here $X(t)$ is the column vector of the unknowns:

$$X(t) = \begin{pmatrix} x_1(t) \\ x_2(t) \\ \cdots \\ x_n(t) \end{pmatrix},$$

$A(t)$ is the $n \times n$ matrix $(a_{i,j})$, and $B(t)$ is the column vector of b_i's. The Existence and Uniqueness theorem for linear systems has a particularly simple form:

Theorem 4.1.1 (Existence and Uniqueness Theorem for linear systems). *Suppose the functions $a_{i,j}(t)$ and $b_i(t)$ are continuous on an interval $c < t < d$. Let X_0 be a column $n-$vector, and $t_0 \in (c, d)$. Then there exists a unique column vector function $X(t)$ defined on all of (c, d) which is a solution of (4.1.2) satisfying the initial condition $X(t_0) = X_0$.*

The system is called **homogeneous** if $B(t)$ is absent. The familiar Superposition Principle says:

Theorem 4.1.2 (Superposition Principle). *Suppose $X_1(t)$ and $X_2(t)$ are two solutions of the homogeneous system of linear equations $X'(t) = AX(t)$. Then*

$$X(t) = c_1 X_1(t) + c_2 X_2(t)$$

is also a solution, for any choice of the constants c_1, c_2. Thus, for any collection of solutions $X_1, \ldots, X_k$ and any choice of constants $c_1, \ldots, c_k$,

$$X(t) = c_1 X_1(t) + c_2 X_2(t) + \cdots + c_k X_k(t)$$

is a solution. In other words, a linear combination of solutions is also a solution.

Let us recall that vector functions $X_1(t), X_2(t), \ldots, X_k(t)$ are **linearly independent** if a linear combination

$$X(t) = c_1 X_1(t) + c_2 X_2(t) + \cdots + c_k X_k(t)$$

is the zero function (that is $X(t) \equiv 0$ or $X(t) = 0$ for every value of t) if and only if all the coefficients are zeros:

$$c_1 = c_2 = \cdots = c_k = 0.$$

Interestingly,

Theorem 4.1.1. *Suppose $X_1(t), X_2(t), \ldots, X_k(t)$ are solutions of a system $X' = AX$. In this case, linear independence of these vector functions is equivalent to linear independence of their values, the vectors $X_1(t_0), \ldots, X_k(t_0)$, at any point t_0.*

It may sound a little confusing, but think about this: it is very easy to produce an example of linearly independent vector functions whose values are linearly dependent at a point. For instance,

$$F_1(t) = \begin{pmatrix} 1 \\ t \end{pmatrix} \text{ and } F_2(t) = \begin{pmatrix} 1 \\ t^2 \end{pmatrix}$$

are linearly independent (can you prove this?). But the vectors $F_1(0)$ and $F_2(0)$ are actually equal, which trivially implies that they are linearly dependent. According to the theorem, this would not be possible for two solutions of the same system. The proof is quite easy.

Proof. It is more convenient to argue that linear dependence of $X_1(t), \ldots, X_k(t)$ is equivalent to linear dependence of $X_1(t_0), \ldots, X_k(t_0)$ at any point t_0. One direction is clear: if there are constants $c_1, \ldots, c_k$ which are not all zeros such that the linear combination

$$X(t) = c_1 X_1(t) + c_2 X_2(t) + \cdots + c_k X_k(t)$$

is the zero function, then $X(t_0) = 0$ for every value t_0, and thus linear dependence of the functions implies linear dependence of their values at a point.

Proving the converse will require using facts about solutions of linear systems. Namely, suppose that a function $X(t)$ defined as above is equal to zero at some value of t:

$$X(t_0) = 0.$$

The Superposition Principle implies that, as a linear combination of solutions, $X(t)$ is also a solution of the system $X' = AX$. On the other hand, the function $Z(t) \equiv 0$ is obviously also a solution, and it satisfies the same initial condition $Z(t_0) = 0$. By the uniqueness part of Existence and Uniqueness Theorem, the two solutions coincide, and thus $X(t)$ is the zero function. □

A corollary of the Superposition Principle and the Existence and Uniqueness Theorem is the following:

> **Theorem 4.1.3.** *Suppose $X' = AX$ is a linear homogeneous system of n equations (that is, A is an $n \times n$ matrix), and let $X_1, \ldots, X_n$ be n linearly independent solutions. Then the general solution of the system can be written as their linear combination, that is, it can be written in the form*
>
> (4.1.3) $\qquad X(t) = c_1 X_1(t) + c_2 X_2(t) + \cdots + c_n X_n(t).$

Proof. By the Existence and Uniqueness Theorem, every solution $X(t)$ is uniquely determined by the choice of an initial value $X_0 = X(t_0)$. We need to demonstrate that any choice of t_0 and X_0 can be realized by a linear combination of the form (4.1.3). Indeed, by Theorem 4.1.1, the vectors $X_1(t_0), X_2(t_0), \ldots, X_n(t_0)$ are linearly independent. Since there are n of them, they form a basis in the n-dimensional space – and thus for any vector X_0, there exists a linear combination

$$c_1 X_1(t_0) + c_2 X_2(t_0) + \cdots + c_n X_n(t_0) = X_0.$$

$\square$

Finally, we have:

Theorem 4.1.4. *Suppose we are given a linear non-homogeneous system of n equations*

(4.1.4) $$X' = AX + B$$

Let

$$X_h(t) = c_1 X_1(t) + c_2 X_2(t) + \cdots + c_n X_n(t)$$

be the general solution (4.1.3) of the corresponding homogeneous system $X' = AX$ (obtained by dropping the vector function B). Furthermore, let X_{nh} be any solution of the non-homogeneous system (a particular solution). Then the general solution of (4.1.4) is given by

$$X = X_h + X_{nh} = c_1 X_1(t) + c_2 X_2(t) + \cdots + c_n X_n(t) + X_{nh}.$$

We say that the system has **constant coefficients** if the entries $a_{i,j}$ in the matrix A are constant. A homogeneous system with constant coefficients has the form

(4.1.5) $$X'(t) = AX(t).$$

This looks like the equation for the exponential growth which we are well familiar with. In fact, *it is* the equation for the exponential growth in the trivial case when $n = 1$. This is a good time to recall the definition of the matrix exponential (1.5.5), and the formula (1.5.6). If we set $W(t) = e^{tA}$, then the whole matrix W satisfies

(4.1.6) $$\frac{d}{dt} W(t) = \frac{d}{dt} e^{tA} = A e^{tA}.$$

This is known as a *fundamental matrix solution*. We can use it to solve the initial value problem

$$X' = AX, \ X(t_0) = X_0$$

as follows. Consider the $n \times n$ matrix $C_0 = e^{-t_0 A} X_0$. Note that

(4.1.7) $$W(t_0) C_0 = e^{t_0 A} e^{-t_0 A} X_0 = I X_0 = X_0.$$

So if we write

(4.1.8) $$X(t) = W(t) C_0,$$

then (4.1.6) and (4.1.7) put together imply that this function is the solution of the initial value problem!

There is only one downside to the above exercise: the formula for the matrix exponential (1.5.5) involves summing an infinite series. This makes the above recipe very difficult to use in practice. Fortunately, a more explicit method of solving linear systems with constant coefficients is available, based on the same type of linear algebra we used for systems of difference equations. Let us start by looking at the case of 2×2 matrices.

4.1.2. Homogeneous linear systems with constant coefficients in dimension 2. As the title says, we will be looking at systems of equations of the familiar form

$$(4.1.9) \qquad\qquad X' = AX$$

when the vector function X has only two components. Rather than labeling them $x_1(t)$, $x_2(t)$, we will usually write

$$X(t) = \begin{pmatrix} x(t) \\ y(t) \end{pmatrix}.$$

Let us note the following. Suppose λ is an eigenvalue of the 2×2 matrix A, and let V be a corresponding eigenvector. Then

$$(4.1.10) \qquad\qquad X(t) = e^{\lambda t} V$$

is a solution of the system (4.1.9). Indeed,

$$AV = \lambda V, \text{ so } AX = \lambda e^{\lambda t} V = (e^{\lambda t})' V = X'.$$

If there are two distinct roots λ_1, λ_2 of the **characteristic equation**

$$|A - \lambda I| = 0,$$

then we get two *linearly independent* solutions

$$X_1(t) = e^{\lambda_1 t} V_1, \ X_2(t) = e^{\lambda_2 t} V_2,$$

where V_i is an eigenvector corresponding to λ_i.

The *general solution* of the system can be written in the form

(4.1.11) $$X(t) = c_1 X_1 + c_2 X_2 = c_1 e^{\lambda_1 t} V_1 + c_2 e^{\lambda_2 t} V_2,$$

where c_1, c_2 are free parameters.

Finally, the values of c_1, c_2 can be obtained from the initial data

$$X(t_0) = X_0.$$

If the characteristic equation has a single root $\lambda_1 = \lambda_2$, then the procedure needs to be modified somewhat. Again, denote V_1 an eigenvector. We say that G is a *generalized eigenvector* if it is a solution of the linear system of equations

(4.1.12) $$(A - \lambda_1 I)G = V_1.$$

In this case, the vector function

(4.1.13) $$X(t) = e^{\lambda_1 t}(tV_1 + G).$$

Thus, the general solution in the case of a repeated eigenvalue has the form:

(4.1.14) $$X(t) = c_1 e^{\lambda_1 t} V_1 + c_2 e^{\lambda_1 t}(tV_1 + G).$$

An example. Consider the system

$$X' = AX$$

with

$$A = \begin{pmatrix} 2 & -1 \\ 1 & 0 \end{pmatrix}$$

The characteristic equation is

$$\begin{vmatrix} 2 - \lambda & -1 \\ 1 & -\lambda \end{vmatrix} = 0,$$

which translates into

$$(\lambda - 1)^2 = 0,$$

so there is a single eigenvalue $\lambda = 1$. We can find an eigenvector

$$V = \begin{pmatrix} v_1 \\ v_2 \end{pmatrix} \text{ from } \begin{pmatrix} 1 & -1 \\ 1 & -1 \end{pmatrix} \begin{pmatrix} v_1 \\ v_2 \end{pmatrix} = 0,$$

or $v_1 = v_2$. We can choose v_1 arbitrarily, let us set $v_1 = 1$, so $v_2 = 1$. Now we need to find a generalized eigenvector G, given by

$$(A - \lambda I)G = V,$$

or

$$\begin{pmatrix} 1 & -1 \\ 1 & -1 \end{pmatrix} \begin{pmatrix} g_1 \\ g_2 \end{pmatrix} = \begin{pmatrix} 1 \\ 1 \end{pmatrix}$$

so that

$$g_1 - g_2 = 1.$$

We can select

$$G = \begin{pmatrix} 2 \\ 1 \end{pmatrix}.$$

The general solution has the form

$$X(t) = c_1 e^{\lambda t} V + c_2 e^{\lambda t} (Vt + G) = c_1 e^t \begin{pmatrix} 1 \\ 1 \end{pmatrix} + c_2 e^t \begin{pmatrix} t+2 \\ t+1 \end{pmatrix}$$

Complex eigenvalues. Finally, let us address the case when the characteristic equation has complex roots $\alpha \pm i\beta$. Of course, the formula (4.1.14) still works, but the functions $X_1(t)$ and $X_2(t)$ will now assume complex values. Since our initial condition $X(t_0) = X_0$ is real, the free parameters c_1, c_2 will also need to be complex. To avoid this, we notice that $X_1(t)$ and $X_2(t)$ are conjugate: $X_1(t) = U(t) + iW(t)$, $X_2(t) = U(t) - iW(t)$. By the Superposition Principle, the real and the imaginary parts

$$U(t) = \text{Re } X_1(t) = \frac{X_1(t) + X_2(t)}{2}, \text{ and } W(t) = \text{Im } X_1(t) = \frac{X_1(t) - X_2(t)}{2i}$$

are also solutions. The general solution can then be written as

$$X(t) = d_1 U(t) + d_2 W(t)$$

with real parameters d_1, d_2.

For example, suppose that the matrix A has an eigenvalue $\lambda_1 = 1 + 2i$ with an eigenvector

$$V_1 = \begin{pmatrix} 3+i \\ 1-4i \end{pmatrix}.$$

From this, we get a solution

$$X_1(t) = e^{(1+2i)t} \begin{pmatrix} 3+i \\ 1-4i \end{pmatrix} = e^t (\cos 2t + i \sin 2t) \begin{pmatrix} 3+i \\ 1-4i \end{pmatrix}.$$

Then

$$U(t) = \text{Re } X_1(t) = \begin{pmatrix} 3e^t \cos 2t - e^t \sin 2t \\ e^t \cos 2t + 4e^t \sin 2t \end{pmatrix},$$

$$W(t) = \text{Im } X_1(t) = \begin{pmatrix} e^t \cos 2t + 3e^t \sin 2t \\ -4e^t \cos 2t + e^t \sin 2t \end{pmatrix},$$

and the general solution is

$$X(t) = d_1 U(t) + d_2 W(t).$$

4.1.3. An application: pharmacokinetic models. As the title of the section suggests, we will mostly use linear systems of differential equations as a tool for understanding non-linear models. But there are some useful models based on them as well. One source of such models is *pharmacokinetics*, which is the study of the movement of drugs within the body. The parts of the body through which a drug passes are seen as separate compartments, and modeling aims to calculate the concentration of the drug in each of the compartments as a function of time. Consider, for instance, a drug which is ingested, and then is absorbed into the bloodstream through the gastrointestinal tract. It is then metabolized in the blood, and cleared out of the body. Let $D(t)$ be the drug dosage (per unit of volume, or weight) as a function of time; let $x(t)$ be the concentration of the drug in the gastrointestinal tract, and let $y(t)$ denote the concentration of the drug in the blood. Consider Figure 18 as an illustration, with $a > b > 0$ being the rates at which the drug is absorbed into the blood, and removed from the body respectively. This basic *two-compartment* pharmacokinetic model is expressed via the following system of differential equations:

(4.1.15)
$$\begin{cases} \dfrac{dx}{dt} = -ax + D(t) \\ \dfrac{dy}{dt} = ax - by \end{cases}$$

The system is not homogeneous, so to solve it, we need to consider a sys-

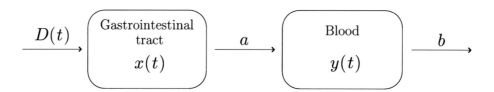

Figure 18. An illustration of a two-compartment pharmacokinetic model.

tem without the external drug input $D(t)$ first:

(4.1.16)
$$\begin{cases} \dfrac{dx}{dt} = -ax \\ \dfrac{dy}{dt} = ax - by \end{cases}$$

It has a matrix

(4.1.17)
$$A = \begin{pmatrix} -a & 0 \\ a & -b \end{pmatrix}$$

whose eigenvalues are $\lambda_1 = -a$, $\lambda_2 = -b$. A corresponding pair of eigenvectors is

$$V_1 = \begin{bmatrix} b - a \\ a \end{bmatrix} \text{ and } V_2 = \begin{bmatrix} 0 \\ 1 \end{bmatrix},$$

so the general solution of the homogeneous system is given by

$$\begin{pmatrix} x(t) \\ y(t) \end{pmatrix} = V_1 = \begin{pmatrix} c_1(b - a)e^{-at} \\ c_1 a e^{-at} + c_2 e^{-bt} \end{pmatrix}$$

Naturally, without an external input of the drug, both concentrations $x(t)$ and $y(t)$ will approach 0 as t increases.

Examples of using the model (4.1.15)
Let us define the system in Maple, using the same notation as in (4.1.15). Well, almost the same notation: I used a lowercase $d(t)$ so that Maple does not confuse it with a derivative.

```
>restart:with(DEtools):
>system1:=diff(x(t),t)=-a*x(t)+d(t),diff(y(t),t)=a*x(t)-b*y(t);
```

Let us quite randomly set
```
>a:=2;b:=1.5;
```

I would like to begin by considering the case when a single dose of a drug was administered at time $t = 1$. This means that $d(t) = 0$ except for a brief interval of time starting at $t = 1$, during which it is a positive constant. There are various ways to define the intake function $d(t)$ to reflect this scenario. I am going to use the step function, which in Maple is called Heaviside(t):

$$\text{Heaviside}(t) = \begin{cases} 0, & t < 0 \\ \text{undefined}, & t = 0 \\ 1, & t > 0 \end{cases}$$

It is quite useful for defining various discontinuous functions. For instance, I can write
```
>d:=t->Heaviside(t-1)-Heaviside(t-2);
```

which corresponds to the administration of a dose of the drug from $t = 1$ to $t = 2$.

Let us assume that initially no drug is present, and solve the system numerically:

```
>ivs:=x(0)=0,y(0)=0;
>solution1:=dsolve([system1,ivs],numeric,output=listprocedure);
```

Maple will say something like
[t=proc(t) ... end proc,x(t)=proc(t) ... end proc,y(t)=proc(t) ... end proc]

We are interested in the function $y(t)$, which is the drug concentration in the blood:

```
>y1:=rhs(solution1[3]);
>plot(y1(t),t=0..10);
```

This will produce the figure

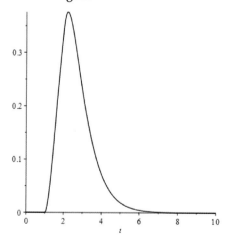

The following function $d(t)$ represents periodic dosing of the drug:

```
d:=t->0.3*Heaviside(cos(t));
```

Using it instead, produces this graph for $y(t)$:

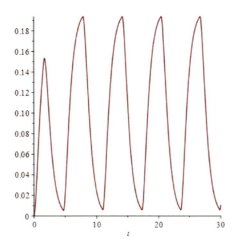

4.1.4. Phase portraits for 2-dimensional linear systems.

Let us start with an example. Consider the system

(4.1.18)
$$\begin{cases} x' = x + 2y \\ y' = 2x + y \end{cases}$$

The matrix

$$A = \begin{bmatrix} 1 & 2 \\ 2 & 1 \end{bmatrix}$$

has the characteristic equation

$$(1 - \lambda)^2 - 4 = 0,$$

which has roots $\lambda_1 = 3$, $\lambda_2 = -1$. Up to a multiplication by a scalar, the eigenvectors for these two eigenvalues are given by

$$V_1 = \begin{bmatrix} 1 \\ 1 \end{bmatrix}, \text{ and } V_2 = \begin{bmatrix} -1 \\ 1 \end{bmatrix} \text{ respectively.}$$

So we can write down the general solution as

$$X(t) = c_1 e^{3t} V_1 + c_2 e^{-t} V_2,$$

where c_1 and c_2 are two free parameters. Written in coordinates, this becomes

(4.1.19)
$$\begin{aligned} x(t) &= c_1 e^{3t} - c_2 e^{-t} \\ y(t) &= c_1 e^{3t} + c_2 e^{-t} \end{aligned}$$

Since a picture is often worth a thousand words, it would be useful to plot the graphs of some of the solutions, as it would help us to understand how the solutions "behave" when t changes. There is an obvious difficulty: the graph of the function $X(t)$ (for given values of the parameters c_1, c_2) is the set of points $(t, x(t), y(t))$, and it is not easy to visualize a curve in three dimensions on a two-dimensional screen. So let us try something different. As you must have seen in Calculus, we can instead only plot the points $(x(t), y(t))$ in the plane, which are obtained by varying t. The Calculus term for this is a *parameterized curve*. In the differential equations jargon, such a curve is called a **trajectory**. The price we pay for switching from a graph in three dimensions to a trajectory in two dimensions is that we can no longer see the dependence on t. If we interpret the independent variable t as the time, then, by looking at a trajectory we not be able to tell *when* a specific point (x, y) on it is visited by the solution. A good parallel, which also helps to explain the term "trajectory", is to think of a white trace of the water vapor that a jet plane leaves in the blue sky overhead. By looking at this trace, we can say "where" the plane was in the sky, but we cannot tell "when". Well, there is one thing we can usually tell – in which direction the plane traveled along its trajectory. A curve can only be traversed in two opposing directions – and we should be able to mark the direction of travel along the curve $(x(t), y(t))$ as t increases.

The Existence and Uniqueness Theorem tells us that there is a single trajectory passing through every point (x_0, y_0) in the plane. Some of these trajectories are easier to visualize than others. To begin with, if $x_0 = 0$ and $y_0 = 0$, then $c_1 = c_2 = 0$, and so one trajectory is a single point, the origin in the plane. By analogy with the one-dimensional case, we will say that $(0, 0)$ is a *fixed point* of our system.

Figure 19. The phase portrait for the system (4.1.18).

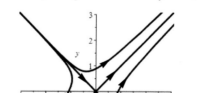

If we set $c_2 = 0$, and $c_1 \neq 0$, then we will obtain anothe special trajectory $X(t) = c_1 e^{3t} V_1$. The scalar e^{3t} spans the interval $(0, +\infty)$ as t goes from $-\infty$ to $+\infty$. If c_1 is positive, then the resulting trajectory is a ray from the origin, along the vector V_1 (see Figure 19). If c_1 is negative, then we get a ray along $-V_1$. We will mark with arrows the direction of travel along these trajectories as t increases. Since e^{3t} is an increasing function of t, the arrows will point away from the origin.

Similarly, if $c_1 = 0$, and $c_2 \neq 0$ then we will get a ray from the origin along the vector V_2, and a ray along $-V_2$. Since e^{-t} is a decreasing function of t, the arrows will point towards the origin along these rays.

In the general case when neither c_1 nor c_2 is equal to 0, it is helpful to think of V_1, V_2 as new unit coordinate vectors (just turn the plane so that V_1 is aligned with the x-axis, and V_2 is aligned with the y-axis to see what I mean). Now the recipe

$$X(t) = c_1 e^{3t} V_1 + c_2 e^{-t} V_2$$

can be interpreted as follows. As t increases, the absolute value of the first coordinate increases, so our point $(x(t), y(t))$ moves further away from the origin along the V_1 axis, and the absolute value of the second coordinate decreases, so $(x(t), y(t))$ moves closer to the origin along the V_2 axis. If the flow of time is reversed $t \to -\infty$, then the opposite happens. The whole trajectory will look like a hyperbola, with asymptotes along the V_1, V_2 axes. The arrows we already have along the axes help to guide us by indicating in which direction we move along the other trajectories as t increases.

In this way, we can get a *qualitative* picture of the behaviour of the trajectories of our system. We will call it a **phase portrait**.

The types of phase portraits we can get for 2-dimensional linear systems with constant coefficients depend on the properties of the eigenvalues. If the characteristic equation

$$|A - \lambda I| = 0$$

has two real roots λ_1, λ_2, and both of them are *negative* then the formula

(4.1.20) $$X(t) = c_1 e^{\lambda_1 t} V_1 + c_2 e^{\lambda_2 t} V_2$$

Figure 20. Phase portraits of linear systems with constant coefficients in 2 dimensions: (a) $\lambda_1 < 0$, $\lambda_2 < 0$; (b) $\lambda_1 > 0$, $\lambda_2 > 0$; (c) $\lambda_1 < 0$, $\lambda_2 > 0$; (d) $\lambda = \alpha \pm i\beta$, $\alpha < 0$; (e) $\lambda = \alpha \pm i\beta$, $\alpha > 0$; (f) $\lambda = \pm i\beta$.

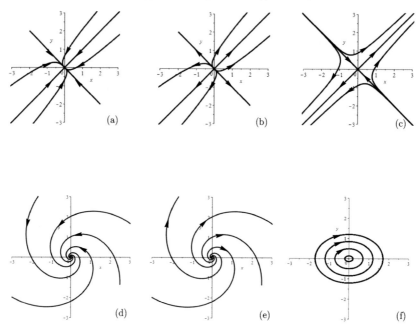

will still give us four special trajectories along rays from the origin in the directions $\pm V_1$, $\pm V_2$, but the arrows along these trajectories will all point towards the origin (as in Figure 20 (a)).

Any other trajectory is obtained by a superposition of the motions along the V_1, V_2 axes as shown in Figure 20 (a). In particular,

$$\lim_{t \to +\infty} X(t) = 0.$$

The case $\lambda_1 > 0$, $\lambda_2 > 0$ is obtained from the previous case by reversing the directions of the arrows, as pictured in Figure 20 (b).

We have already dealt with the situation when λ_1 and λ_2 have opposite signs (Figure 20 (c)).

The case when $\lambda_1 = \lambda_2$ will look similar to Figure 20 (a) or (b) depending on whether $\lambda_1 < 0$ or $\lambda_1 > 0$. The only difference is that there will only be one pair straight-ray trajectories, along $\pm V_1$.

In remains to discuss the case when there are two complex conjugate roots of the characteristic equation

$$\lambda = \alpha \pm i\beta.$$

Let us denote V_1 the eigenvector corresponding to $\lambda_1 = \alpha + i\beta$. Since the eigenvalue is complex, the eigenvector V_1 will have a real and an imaginary parts:

$$V_1 = K + iL.$$

We can write

$$X_1(t) = e^{\lambda_1 t} V_1 = e^{(\alpha + i\beta)t}(K + iL) = e^{\alpha t} e^{i\beta t}(K + iL).$$

Using the Euler's formula, we get

$$X_1(t) = e^{\alpha t}(\cos(\beta t) + i\sin(\beta t))(K + iL).$$

We see that

$$
\begin{aligned}
U(t) &= \operatorname{Re} X_1(t) = e^{\alpha t}(K\cos(\beta t) - L\sin(\beta t)) \text{ and}\\
W(t) &= \operatorname{Im} X_1(t) = e^{\alpha t}(K\sin(\beta t) + L\cos(\beta t)).
\end{aligned}
$$

What do the trajectories given by

$$X(t) = d_1 U(t) + d_2 W(t)$$

look like? Both for $U(t)$ and for $W(t)$ the expressions inside the parentheses are periodic with period $2\pi/\beta$. In the case when $\alpha = 0$ the function $X(t)$ will be periodic, and so the trajectories will close up into loops, traversed in time $t = 2\pi/\beta$. It is possible to show that these loops will be shaped as concentric ellipses around the origin (Figure 20 (f)).

If $\operatorname{Re}\lambda_1 = \alpha < 0$, then the amplitude of the periodic oscillations in the parantheses will be multiplied by the quantity $e^{\alpha t}$ which *decreases* with time. In this case, the trajectories will look as spirals (Figure 20 (d)), with arrows pointed towards the origin:

$$\lim_{t \to +\infty} X(t) = 0.$$

Finally, in Figure 20 (e), we see the case $\alpha > 0$. It looks just like the previous case, but with arrows pointed away from the origin:

$$\lim_{t \to -\infty} X(t) = 0 \text{ and } \lim_{t \to +\infty} X(t) = \infty.$$

4.1.5. Higher dimensional linear systems. What about higher dimensional systems? As in the two-dimensional case, if λ is an eigenvalue of an $n \times n$ matrix A, and V is a corresponding eigenvector, then

$$x(t) = e^{\lambda t} V$$

is a solution of the system $X' = AX$. If there are n linearly independent solutions of this form, then the general solution is given by their linear combination. If not, then extra solutions can be found using generalized eigenvectors – but it gets too technical, so we will not discuss it here, and refer to any standard text on Differential Equations instead. And, of course, plotting solutions or trajectories becomes impossible in higher dimensions (although we can still try to visualize their two-dimensional projections, which may sometimes be useful).

4.2. Nonlinear systems

4.2.1. Getting ready to tackle nonlinear systems: Existence and Uniqueness Theorem. A general n-dimensional system of first-order differential equations has the form

$$X'(t) = F(t, X(t)),$$

where the unknown X is a column n-vector function, and F is a function $\mathbb{R}^{n+1} \to \mathbb{R}^n$. We are only going to look at **autonomous** systems, which have the form

$$(4.2.1) \qquad\qquad\qquad X' = F(X),$$

so the right-hand side does not depend on the value of t. In coordinates, we will write

$$X = \begin{pmatrix} x_1 \\ x_2 \\ \dots \\ x_n \end{pmatrix} \quad \text{and } F(X) = \begin{pmatrix} f_1(x_1, \dots, x_n) \\ f_2(x_1, \dots, x_n) \\ \dots \\ f_n(x_1, \dots, x_n) \end{pmatrix}$$

Let us put on our Calculus hats, and make a substitution $\tau = t + T$ (resetting the clock by T units of time). Since $\tau'(t) = 1$, we end up with the same system

$$X'(\tau) = F(X(\tau)).$$

What this simple exercise tells us is that if $X(t)$ is a solution of an autonomous system, then so is $X(t + T)$.

The Existence and Uniqueness Theorem for autonomous systems is going to look very familiar:

Theorem 4.2.1. *Suppose there exists an n-dimensional cube*

$$C = (a_1, b_1) \times (a_2, b_2) \times \cdots \times (a_n, b_n)$$

such that at every point $X \in C$ the function F is continuous and has continuous partial derivatives $\partial f_i / \partial x_j$. Let $X_0 \in C$. Then the initial value problem

$$X' = F(x), \; X(t_0) = X_0$$

has a unique solution on some interval $(t_0 - \epsilon, t_0 + \epsilon)$.

Furthermore, if $C = \mathbb{R}^n$ and, furthermore, the partial derivatives of F are bounded in $\mathbb{R}^n$, then $X(t)$ is defined for all $t \in (-\infty, +\infty)$.

In two dimensions, the system (4.2.1) takes the form

$$\begin{cases} x' = f(x,y) \\ y' = g(x,y) \end{cases}$$

In the same way as we did for the linear systems, we will view a solution $(x(t), y(t))$ as a parametrized curve in the plane, and will call it a *trajectory*. Note an important consequence of Existence and Uniqueness Theorem 4.2.1:

if two trajectories intersect at a point $(x_0, y_0) \in \mathbb{R}^2$, then they must coincide.

Indeed, by resetting the time for one of the solutions, we can ensure that both of the trajectories satisfy the same initial conditions $x(t_0) = x_0, y(t_0) = y_0$ – and then use the uniqueness part of the theorem.

4.2.2. Equilibrium point analysis of systems of differential equations. By a direct analogy with the one-dimensional situation, let us say that X_0 is an **equilibrium point** of (4.2.1) if $F(X_0) = 0$. Equivalently,

$$X(t) \equiv X_0$$

is a solution, which we again call an **equilibrium solution**. Recall, that our analysis of phase diagrams in one dimension was based on the study of the equilibrium solutions (see Theorem 3.2.1). Can we do something similar in n dimensions? Let us start with the familar case of $n = 2$. What will the trajectories of the system look like near an equilibrium point?

We can get some intuition from looking at the case when the right-hand side in (4.2.1) is linear, with constant coefficients:

$$X' = AX.$$

For a linear system, there is always at least one equilibrium point:

$$X_0 = 0,$$

and we can look at Figure 20 to see how the trajectories behave near this point. In the cases (a), (d), for example, all arrows lead to 0. Equilibria in these cases should definitely be classified as stable, by analogy with the one-dimensional picture. But there is another scenario which also deserves the name "stable", which is absent in one dimension. I am talking about case (f), when nearby trajectories do not converge to 0, but forever remain in its close vicinity. Let us make an important general definition:

Definition 4.2.1. Suppose X_0 is an equilibrium point of $X' = F(X)$. We say that it is a **stable** equilibrium if for every $\epsilon > 0$ there exists $\delta > 0$ such that if $\text{dist}(X_1, X_0) < \delta$, and $X(t)$ is a solution which satisfies the initial condition $X(t_1) = X_1$, the *for all $t > t_1$* we have

$$\text{dist}(X(t), X_0) < \epsilon.$$

Ah, this is like one of those dreaded ϵ-δ definitions from Calculus. We can decypher it as follows: we can guarantee that a trajectory will stay as close to X_0 as we would like to for all future time (ϵ-close), by choosing its starting point sufficiently close (δ-close). See, now it all makes sense. The opposite of stable will be called **unstable**, like in the 1-dimensional case.

By the above definition, we have three cases when 0 is a stable equilibrium of a two-dimensional linear system $X' = AX$:

- *A* has two real (possibly equal) eigenvalues $\lambda_1 < 0$, $\lambda_2 < 0$ (case (a) in Figure 20;
- *A* has two complex conjugate eigenvalues $\lambda = \alpha \pm i\beta$ and the real part $\alpha < 0$ (case (d) in Figure 20;
- *A* has two imaginary eigenvalues $\lambda = \pm i\beta$ (case (f) in Figure 20.

We could be extra slick and simply say 0 is stable if for every eigenvalue λ, the real part $\text{Re}\,\lambda \leq 0$, but it obscures the case that we have three different phase portraits here with different types of behaviour. What sets the first two possibilities apart is that the trajectories actually converge to 0. Let us make another definition:

Definition 4.2.2. Suppose X_0 is an equilibrium point of $X' = F(X)$. We say that it is **attracting** if there exists $\delta > 0$ such that if $\text{dist}(X_1, X_0) < \delta$, and $X(t)$ is a solution which satisfies the initial condition $X(t_1) = X_1$, then

$$\lim_{t \to +\infty} X(t) = X_0.$$

Similarly,

Definition 4.2.3. An equilibrium point X_0 is **repelling** if there exists $\delta > 0$ such that if $\text{dist}(X_1, X_0) < \delta$, and $X(t)$ is a solution which satisfies the initial condition $X(t_1) = X_1$, then

$$\lim_{t \to -\infty} X(t) = X_0.$$

To distinguish the portraits (a) and (d) in Figure 20, we will say that an equilibrium point X_0 is a **node**, if there is a trajectory tangent to a straight line through X_0. A stable node will be called, well, you guessed it, a **stable node**. An attracting point which is not a node (like in portrait (d)) will be known as a **stable spiral point**. A stable point which is not attracting (case (f)) will be called a **center**.

For repelling point, the corresponding terms will be an **unstable node**, and an **unstable spiral point**.

Finally, a node may be neither attracting, nor repelling, like in portrait (c), in which there are two trajectories which converge to 0 for $t \to +\infty$, and two more, which converge to 0 for $t \to -\infty$. We will call such a point a **saddle node**; it is obviously unstable.

Why "saddle"? Place an actual saddle on a horizontal surface, put a golf ball on top of the saddle, and as the ball is rolling over the saddle, mark its trajectory on the surface below. As is seen in the schematic Figure 21, there is a spot in the middle of the saddle, where the ball would rest in a (precarious) balance. If you carefully place the ball anywhere else on the middle ridge along the top of the saddle (marked with a solid white line in the figure), then it will roll towards the middle. On the two-dimensional surface below, this will correspond to two straight line trajectories pointing towards the equilibrium point. There are two ortogonal trajectories pointing away from the equilibrium, corresponding to the ball rolling off in the middle of the sides of the saddle. If you place the ball anywhere else, it will also roll

Figure 21. Why "saddle"? A schematic illustration.

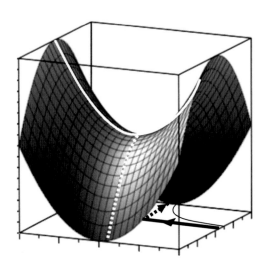

off the saddle, along a trajectory which looks like a hyperbola on the plane below the saddle.

We thus have the following classification of $2D$ linear phase portraits in Figure 20 depending on the eigenvalues λ_1, λ_2 of the matrix A:

- $\lambda_1 < 0, \lambda_2 < 0$: a **stable node** (a);
- $\lambda_1 > 0, \lambda_2 > 0$: an **unstable node** (b);
- $\lambda_1 < 0 < \lambda_2$: a **saddle node** (c);
- $\lambda_{1,2} = \alpha \pm i\beta, \alpha < 0, \beta \neq 0$: a **stable spiral point** (d);
- $\lambda_{1,2} = \alpha \pm i\beta, \alpha > 0, \beta \neq 0$: an **unstable spiral point** (e);
- $\lambda_{1,2} = \pm i\beta, \beta \neq 0$: a **center** (f).

A useful shortcut. Suppose the matrix A of the linear system $X' = AX$ has the form

$$A = \begin{pmatrix} a & b \\ c & d \end{pmatrix}.$$

Let us denote the determinant of A by

$$\Delta = ad - bc,$$

and let us recall that the *trace* τ of A is the sum of the diagonal elements

$$\tau = a + d.$$

The characteristic equation

$$\begin{vmatrix} a - \lambda & b \\ c & d - \lambda \end{vmatrix} = 0,$$

or

$$\lambda^2 - \lambda(a + d) + (ad - bc) = 0,$$

which translates into

(4.2.2) $$\lambda^2 - \tau\lambda + \Delta = 0.$$

Its roots are given by the quadratic formula:

(4.2.3) $$\lambda = \frac{\tau \pm \sqrt{\tau^2 - 4\Delta}}{2}.$$

We see that:

- The system $X' = AX$ has a saddle node if and only if $\Delta < 0$.
- If $\Delta > 0$ and $\tau < 0$, the system has a stable node or a stable spiral point.
- If $\Delta > 0$ and $\tau > 0$, the system has an unstable node or an unstable spiral point.
- Finally, the system has a center if $\Delta > 0$ and $\tau = 0$.

Indeed, if $\Delta < 0$ then $\sqrt{\tau^2 - 4\Delta}$ is a real number greater than $|\tau|$, so one of the roots of the characteristic equation will be positive, and the other one negative.

If $\Delta > 0$, consider first the case when $4\Delta > \tau^2$. Then, $\lambda = \alpha \pm i\beta$ with $\beta \neq 0$ and $\alpha = \tau/2$. So the equilibrium point at 0 is an unstable spiral point, a stable spiral point, or a center when respectively $\tau > 0$, $\tau < 0$, and $\tau = 0$. In the remaining case when $4\Delta \in (0, \tau^2]$, the square root

$$\sqrt{\tau^2 - 4\Delta} \in [0, |\tau|),$$

so if $\tau > 0$ then both eigenvalues are positive, and if $\tau < 0$ then both are negative.

Equilibrium points of non-linear systems. What comes next is the main reason we studied linear systems, and the key to understanding non-linear phase portraits in two dimensions.

Recall that the **Jacobi matrix**, or simply the **Jacobian**, of the two-dimensional function

$$F(x,y) = \left(\begin{array}{c} f(x,y) \\ g(x,y) \end{array} \right)$$

is the matrix of its partial derivatives

$$\mathrm{Jac}_{x,y} = \left(\begin{array}{cc} \dfrac{\partial f}{\partial x}(x,y) & \dfrac{\partial f}{\partial y}(x,y) \\[3mm] \dfrac{\partial g}{\partial x}(x,y) & \dfrac{\partial g}{\partial y}(x,y) \end{array} \right)$$

Let us write a two-dimensional nonlinear system $X' = F(X)$ out in coordinates:

(4.2.4)
$$\begin{cases} x' = f(x,y) \\ y' = g(x,y) \end{cases}$$

and suppose that (x_0, y_0) is an equilibrium point, so that $f(x_0, y_0) = g(x_0, y_0) = 0$.

Definition 4.2.4. The **linearization** of the nonlinear system (4.2.4) at the equilibrium (x_0, y_0) is the linear system with constant coefficients whose matrix $A = \mathrm{Jac}_{x_0, y_0}$ is the Jacobian of F at the equilibrium point.

The linearization captures the behaviour of the nonlinear system near the equilibrium point as follows:

Theorem 4.2.1 (Linearization of nonlinear systems). *Suppose $X' = AX$ is the linearization of a two-dimensional nonlinear system $X' = F(X)$ at (x_0, y_0). Denote λ_1, λ_2 the eigenvalues of the matrix $A = \mathrm{Jac}_{x_0, y_0}$. The the following is true:*

- *Suppose the equilibrium $(0,0)$ of the linear system is a stable or an unstable node, a stable or an unstable spiral point, or a saddle node. If $\lambda_1 \neq \lambda_2$, then the type of the equilibrium (x_0, y_0) of the nonlinear system is the same. In particular, the phase portrait of the nonlinear system near (x_0, y_0) looks the same as the phase portrait of the linear system near $(0,0)$.*
- *If the linear system has a stable or an unstable node and $\lambda_1 = \lambda_2$, then the stability of the equilibrium (x_0, y_0) is the same as that of the equilibrium $(0,0)$ of the linearization, but it may be either a node or a spiral point.*

In short, the phase portrait near the equilibrium point of the nonlinear system looks like the corresponding phase portrait for the linearization from Figure 20 in all cases **except case (f), when the linearized system has a center.** One minor change is possible in case when $\lambda_1 = \lambda_2$: the nonlinear system may have a spiral point instead of a node. If the linearized system has a center, then the linearization approach fails – we do not get any useful information about the equilibrium of the nonlinear system.

4.2.3. A tiny bit more theory before the fun begins. Here is another observation which can help us visualize a trajectory $(x(t), y(t))$ of a two-dimensional system

$$\begin{cases} x' = f(x, y) \\ y' = g(x, y) \end{cases}$$

The slope of the parametrized curve $(x(t), y(t))$ can be found using the Chain Rule:

$$\frac{dy}{dx} = \frac{dx/dt}{dy/dt} = \frac{g(x, y)}{f(x, y)}.$$

The ratio $g(x, y)/f(x, y)$ defines a **slope field** in the plane, which the trajectories fit.

Let us make a useful definition:

Definition 4.2.5. The **x-nullcline** is the set of points given by $\{f(x, y) = 0\}$. Similarly, the **y-nullcline** is the set of points given by $\{g(x, y) = 0\}$.

The x-nullcline is the set of points on which $x'(t) = 0$. When a trajectory crosses the x-nullcline, its slope is vertical. The x-nullcline separates the regions in which the trajectories go right ($x' > 0$) from the regions where they go left ($x' < 0$). Similarly, the y-nullcline separates the regions where the trajectories go up ($y' > 0$) from the ones where they go down ($y' < 0$). On the y-nullcline itself, the slope field is horizontal. Note that the equilibrium points are the intersections of the x- and y-nullclines.

Let us look at an example:

(4.2.5)
$$\begin{cases} x' = 1 - xy \\ y' = x^3 - y \end{cases}$$

We illustrate it The x-nullcline is the hyperbola $y = 1/x$, and the y-nullcline is the cubic $y = x^3$, as seen in Figure 22. Their intersections are

Figure 22. The nullclines of the system (4.2.5). The arrows mark the direction of the slope field

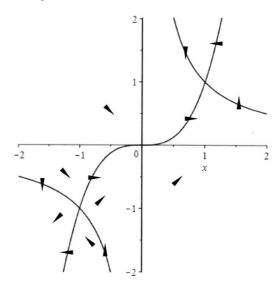

the two equilibrium points of the system $(-1, -1)$ and $(1, 1)$. The two nullclines partition the plane in the regions in which the left-right and up-down directions of the trajectories are the same. It is helpful to put arrows on the nullclines themeselves to indicate the direction of the trajectories as they cross them. For instance, the arrows are horizontal on the y-nullcline; the x-nullcline cuts it into three pieces, and the arrows point right on the middle piece, and left on the other two. After we have put the arrows on the x- and y-nullcline, combining them in each of the sectors they cut the plane into is straightforward (see the Figure). As an illustration of the information we can get from this, look at the arrows I have put around the equilibrium point $(-1, -1)$. Can you compare this with our zoo of phase portraits in Figure 20 and figure out what the type of this equilibroum is? Spoiler: it is a saddle node.

4.3. Let the fun begin: models of ecosystems with several species

4.3.1. Competing species. Our introduction into the world of serious non-linear modeling comes from the following scenario. We consider an ecosystem with limited resources in which there are two species, a population $x(t)$ and a population $y(t)$, which compete with each other for the survival. To describe a single population in an ecosystem with a limit on resources, we have previously used the logistic model (3.1.10). So, for instance, if no members of the second species are present (that is, $y(t) = 0$), then the equation for x would have the form

$$x' = kx(M - x).$$

Adding y's should have a negative effect on the availability of resources, and supress the growth rate. The simplest equation to describe such an effect would incorporate a negative linear term $-ay$ in parentheses:

$$x' = kx(M - x - ay).$$

Doing the same for the second species, we obtain a system of two equations:

(4.3.1)
$$\begin{cases} x' = kx(M - x - ay) \\ y' = ly(N - y - bx) \end{cases}$$

The x-nullcline is the y-axis $x = 0$ and the line $M - x - ay = 0$; the y-nullcline is the x-axis $y = 0$ and the line $N - y - bx = 0$. There are three "uninteresting" equilibrium points:

- $(0,0)$ neither of the species present in the ecosystem;
- $(M,0)$ the first is present, the second is not;
- $(0, N)$ the second is present, the first is not.

Finally, there may be a case when the lines $M - x - ay = 0$ and $N - y - bx = 0$ intersect at a point (x_*, y_*) in the first quadrant (we are only interested in the first quadrant, since, clearly, negative values of x and y do not make sense in our model).

Let us look at a specific example:

(4.3.2)
$$\begin{cases} x' = x(3 - x - 2y) \\ y' = y(2 - y - x) \end{cases}$$

Here the equilibrium points are $(0,0)$, $(3,0)$, $(0,2)$, and $(1,1)$. The x-nullcline is the y-axis $x = 0$ and the line $3 - x - 2y = 0$; the y-nullcline is the x-axis $y = 0$ and the line $2 - y - x = 0$ (see Figure 23)). Each of the axes corresponds to the absence of one of the species. Thus we have a copy of the familiar one-dimensional logistic phase diagram (11) on each of the axes. Along the positive x-axis, the arrows lead to $(3,0)$, and along the positive

Figure 23. Nullclines for the system (4.3.2). Two thicker lines are the x-nullcline; two thinner ones are the y-nullcline.

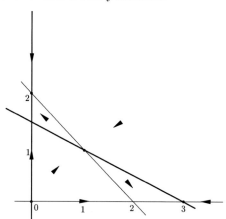

y-axis the arrows lead to $(0,2)$. Looking at our zoo of linearized phase portraits (Figure 20), we see that $(0,0)$ is an unstable node. Both $(3,0)$ and $(0,2)$ are nodes, and they can be either stable nodes or saddle nodes.

The key to undestanding the phase portrait is the analysis of the "interesting" equilibrium point $(1,1)$. The Jacobi matrix at this point is given by

$$\text{Jac}_{1,1} = \begin{pmatrix} -1 & -2 \\ -1 & -1 \end{pmatrix}$$

The eigenvalues of this matrix are $1 \pm \sqrt{2}$, so the point $(1,1)$ is a saddle node. Alas, it is unstable, so the two species will not stably coexist.

Linearizing at the other two equilibrium points $(3,0)$, $(0,2)$ we see that both of them are stable nodes (verify this by yourself!).

Putting together the whole phase portrait is more art than science, but here is a helpful strategy. Start with the saddle(s) in the picture (well, we only have one). A saddle will have four trajectories ending there, two going out opposite each other, and two going in similarly opposite each other. The former are known as *unstable separatrices*, and the latter are known as *stable separatrices* – separatrices, since they separate the plane into sectors. We can try to draw the separatrices, and particularly, try to connect them to the other equilibrium points. The arrows marking the slope field tell us what we should do. The unstable separatrices connect the saddle $(1,1)$

Figure 24. The phase portrait of the system (4.3.2).

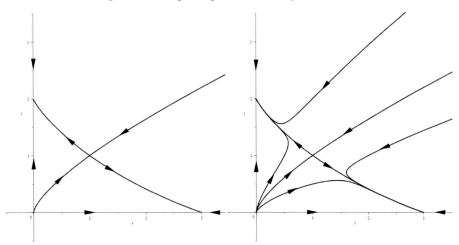

with the two attracting points $(3,0)$ and $(0,2)$ (see Figure 24, left). One of the stable ones connects the point $(0,0)$ with $(1,1)$, and the other one has nowhere left to connect to, so its other end will go off to infinity.

Having put the separatrices down, we should be able to complete the picture (see Figure 24, right). The other trajectories now have to agree with the direction and the position of the separatrices. We see that the two stable separatrices are particularly important: they divide the first quadrant into the lower half, in which all trajectories converge to $(3,0)$ – and so the first species wins, and the second one goes extinct; and the upper half in which the first species goes extinct, and trajectories converge to $(2,0)$. The threshold behaviour of converging to the unstable equilibrium $(1,1)$ will not happen in practice – sooner or later the numbers will deviate ever so slightly from this curve, pushing one of the two species to extinction.

Using a computer algebra system for plotting a few trajectories is relatively straightforward. In *Maple,* we would first load the package **DEtools,** and enter the equations of the system (4.3.2):

```
>with(DEtools):
>system1:=diff(x(t),t)=x(t)*(3-x(t)-2*y(t)),
         diff(y(t),t)=y(t)*(2-y(t)-x(t));
```

We can then use the command **DEplot** to plot the trajectories, starting at the initial values (x_0, y_0) of our choice. But how can we choose an initial value which lies on a stable (or an unstable) separatrix of the saddle point $(1,1)$? Pinpointing an exact location of a curve in the plane seems like an impossible task - and indeed, it is. Whatever initial point we pick, no matter how good a guess it is, the trajectory starting there will most certainly miss $(1,1)$. So here is a pro tip: if we pick an initial point very close to $(1,1)$, then the trajectory will follow very close to an unstable separatrix in forward time, and to a stable separatrix in backward time. It will turn the corner at $(1,1)$ so tightly, that in practice it will be hard to distinguish from the pair of separatrices. Following this recipe, the code I used to plot the curves in Figure 24, left is:

```
>DEplot({system1},[x(t),y(t)],-30..30,{[0,1.002,1],[0,0.998,1]},
        x=0..3,y=0..3,stepsize=0.03,arrows=none,linecolor=black);
```

Let us now consider a modified example:

$$(4.3.3) \qquad \begin{cases} x' = x(3 - 2x - y) \\ y' = y(2 - y - x) \end{cases}$$

Here, the fixed points are $(0,0)$, $(1.5,0)$, $(0,2)$, and $(1,1)$. Linearization shows that $(1,1)$ is a stable node, guranteeing peaceful and happy coexistence of the two species. The points $(1.5,0)$, $(0,2)$ turn into saddles, their unstable separatrices connect them to $(1,1)$, as shown in Figure 25. Can you complete the drawing, showing other typical trajectories?

Figure 25. The separatrices in the phase portrait of the system(4.3.3).

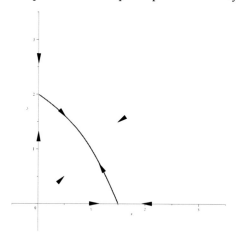

The above discussion is our first complete analysis of a nonlinear model in dimension 2. On the one hand, it is clearly successful: there are two qualitatively different behaviours on the model, depending on the stability of the equilibrium point (x_*, y_*) and we can describe the long-term scenarios for both of these behaviours. On the other hand, the analysis is a lot less straightforward than in dimension 1. There is no clear recipe for drawing a phase portrait, and it is not obvious, in particular, what types of behaviour we should expect in general from two-dimensional trajectories. We will shed some light on this question in the next section. In the meantime, let us look at another ecological model.

4.3.2. A predator-prey model. Consider the following system of equations describing an interaction between two species:

(4.3.4)
$$\begin{cases} x' = kx(M - x - ay) \\ y' = ly(-N - y + bx) \end{cases}$$

where all of the constants are positive. Compare it with the system (4.3.1) describing an ecosystem with two competing species. The differences are the minus sign in front of N and the plus sign in front of bx in the second equation. In (4.3.4) the first of the species, whose number is given by $x(t)$, is prey to the second one. In the absence of the predators ($y = 0$), the first equation turns into the usual logistic population model. In the absence of prey ($x = 0$), predators die out from starvation, which explains the sign of $-N$. On the other hand, the presence of prey is beneficial to the predators, which is why x enters the second equation with a positive coefficient.

Let us analyze a specific example:

(4.3.5)
$$\begin{cases} x' = x(2 - x - y) \\ y' = y(-1 - y + 2x) \end{cases}$$

The equilibrium points are $(0,0)$, $(2,0)$, $(1,1)$, and $(0,-1)$, however, the last of them has a negative value of y so it is not biologically relevant and we will exclude it from our analysis. The Jacobian is

$$\text{Jac}_{x,y} = \begin{pmatrix} 2 - y - 2x & -x \\ 2y & -1 + 2x - 2y \end{pmatrix}$$

At the "interesting" equilibrium $(1,1)$, we have

$$\text{Jac}_{1,1} = \begin{pmatrix} -1 & -1 \\ 2 & -1 \end{pmatrix}$$

The characteristic equation is

$$(\lambda + 1)^2 + 2 = 0.$$

Its roots are $\lambda = -1 \pm i\sqrt{2}$, so this is a stable spiral point.

$$\mathrm{Jac}_{2,0} = \begin{pmatrix} -2 & -2 \\ 0 & 3 \end{pmatrix}$$

Its eigenvalues are -2 and 3, so this equilibrium point is a saddle (and thus unstable). In the absence of the predators ($y = 0$), the system turns into a one-dimensional logistic model which "lives" on the x-axis; the point $x = 2$ is the limiting stable population for this model.

Finally, the point $(0,0)$ is also a saddle. A quick way to see it is as follows. Along the x-axis (no predators) the system is described by a logistic model, in which 0 is the unstable equilibrium. Thus, the arrow points *away* from the origin along the positive horizontal axis. If $y = 0$ (no prey), predators will starve, and thus the arrow points *towards* the origin along the positive vertical axis. These are the hallmarks of a saddle. We can verify this using the Jacobian as well:

$$\mathrm{Jac}_{0,0} = \begin{pmatrix} 2 & 0 \\ 0 & -1 \end{pmatrix}$$

which is a diagonal matrix with eigenvalues 2 and -1.

A phase plot is seen in Figure 26. To connect the "dots" in this picture, I first put the arrows on the positive x- and y-axes, as discussed above. Next, an unstable separatrix of the saddle $(2,0)$ terminates at $(1,1)$. Other trajectories in the first quadrant follow the traffic rules set out by the separatrices.

A historical note. Ecological models of the type we have considered above are known as *Lotka Volterra* systems. To appreciate the variety of ecological models of several interacting species have a look at the book [**Baz98**]. It contains a systematic description of possible modes of interaction, and the resulting systems of differential equations. Such systems are the mainstay of ecological modeling. The original works of A.J. Lotka and V. Volterra concerned a form of the predator-prey system, somewhat simpler than the one we have considered above. Lotka analyzed this system in his book on mathematical biology [**Lot25**] (sort of like this one). Volterra independently developed the model to explain fluctuations in the size of the catch of predatory fish in the Adriatic sea [**Vol26**] – possibly the first application of non-linear differential equations to explain an ecological phenomenon.

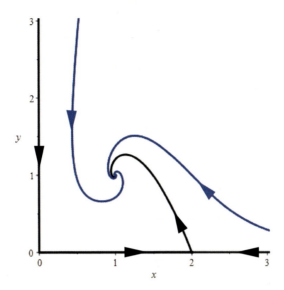

Figure 26. Phase portrait for system (5.4.3). Separatrices are in black, typical trajectories in blue.

**Exercises for
Chapter 4**

1. 💡 **Linear (in)dependence of functions.**

   (a) Prove that the vector functions

   $$F_1 = \begin{pmatrix} 1 \\ t \end{pmatrix} \text{ and } F_2 = \begin{pmatrix} 1 \\ t^2 \end{pmatrix}$$

   are linearly independent.

   (b) Prove that for any non-negative integer N, the power functions

   $$f_0(t) = 1, f_1(t) = t, f_2(t) = t^2, \ldots, f_N(t) = t^N$$

   are linearly independent.
   You are already familiar with this statement in a different form: a polynomial

   $$P(t) = c_0 + c_1 t + c_2 t^2 + \cdots + c_N t^N$$

   is equal to 0 for all values of t if and only if

   $$c_0 = c_1 = \cdots = c_N = 0.$$

2. Finish example (4.2.5): linearize the system at each of the equilibrium points, determine their type and stability, and sketch the phase portrait of the system indicating typical trajectories.

3. **More of the same.** For each of the two dimensional systems below do the following:

   - find the equilibrium points;
   - find the nullclines, sketch them, and indicate with arrows the directions of the trajectories in each of the sectors between the nullclines;
   - for each of the equilibrium points find the linearization of the system, to determine its type and the stability;
   - sketch a possible phase portrait, indicating the typical trajectories.

   (a)

   $$\begin{cases} x' = 2x - 2xy \\ y' = 2 - y - x \end{cases}$$

(b)
$$\begin{cases} x' = x - xy \\ y' = -y + y^2x \end{cases}$$

4. A model of two competing species in an ecosystem is given by the following system of differential equations:

$$\begin{cases} x' = x(1 - x - y) \\ y' = y(0.75 - y - 0.5x) \end{cases}$$

Find the equilibrium points of the system. Use linearization to determine whether the system predicts peaceful coexistence of the two species or extinction of one of them. Draw a phase portrait indicating the equilibrium points and some typical trajectories.

5. A rabbit population in Australia was started with less than a dozen European rabbits. Favourable conditions (mild winters, flat landscape, lack of natural predators) allowed the rabbit population to multiply exponentially and seriously damaged the local ecology. In their original habitat, the number of rabbits is bounded because of their natural predators (foxes, wolves, lynx, etc.) so that the predator-prey system reaches an ecological balance.

Five red foxes were then released in Australia to start a fox population and fix the disbalance. Nonetheless, the number of rabbits continued to grow (until it was finally brought under control by an introduction of a deadly rabbit virus). It is interesting that the population of foxes also grew and began to present a danger too. One of the possible ways to explain why it happened is to use a predator-prey system which takes into account competition between predators, and saturation (there is a limit on how much rabbit meat a fox could eat):

$$\begin{cases} u' = u - \dfrac{uv}{(1+\alpha u)(1+\beta v)} \\[3mm] v' = -v + \dfrac{uv}{(1+\alpha u)(1+\beta v)} \end{cases}$$

here $\alpha > 0, \beta > 0$.

(a) Consider the case $\alpha = \beta = 0.2$. Find all of the equilibrium points of the system. Linearize the system at these points: does the linearization tell you the type and the stability of each of them?

(b) Use a computer algebra system to draw a phase portrait for $\alpha = \beta = 0.2$ and try to explain why the number of rabbits $u(t)$ (in millions) was growing even after foxes appeared, $v(t)$ is the number of foxes (in hundreds).

6. A population of orcas (killer whales) is not viable if its numbers drop below a certain minimum threshold. An example of a one-dimensional model describing such a population is a modification of the logistic model given by

$$x' = rx(x - L)(M - x) \text{ with } r, L, M > 0,$$

where L is the minimum survival threshold.

Orcas compete with seals for wild salmon. Consider a system describing the competition between orcas, whose numbers $x(t)$ (in hundreds) follow the above model, and seals, whose numbers $y(t)$ (in thousands) follow the usual logistic model:

$$\begin{cases} x' = 2x(x - 2)(4 - x) - xy \\ y' = y(5 - y) - xy \end{cases}$$

(a) Find the equilibrium points of the system. Linearize the system at these points and determine their type and stability.

(b) Sketch a phase portrait, mark all of the separatrices of the system. In the phase portrait, indicate the region of initial conditions for which the population of orcas will survive over time.

References for Chapter 4

[Baz98]   A.D. Bazykin, *Nonlinear Dynamics of Interacting Populations*, Edited by: A.I. Khibnik, Bernd Krauskopf. World Scientific Series on Nonlinear Science Series A: Volume 11(1998), 216pp.

[Lot25]   Lotka, A. J. *Elements of Physical Biology*. Williams and Wilkins, 1925

[Vol26]   Volterra, V. *Variazioni e fluttuazioni del numero d'individui in specie animali conviventi*. Mem. Acad. Lincei Roma. 2(1926), 31–113.

Two dimensional non-linear models, from alpha to omega

5.1. Understanding the long-term behavior of a two-dimensional model

5.1.1. Periodic trajectories and limit cycles. We will need to make some definitions. Consider the autonomous system of differential equations given by

(5.1.1)
$$\begin{cases} x' = f(x,y) \\ y' = g(x,y) \end{cases}$$

such that f and g are continuous and have continuous and bounded partial derivatives in $\mathbb{R}^2$.

Definition 5.1.1. Let $(x(t), y(t))$ be a trajectory of the system (5.1.1) satisfying the initial condition $x(t_0) = x_0$, $y(t_0) = y_0$. We say that (x_*, y_*) is an **ω-limit point** of (x_0, y_0) if there exists a sequence $t_k \to +\infty$ such that

$$\lim_{k \to \infty} (x(t_k), y(t_k)) = (x_*, y_*).$$

Similarly, We say that (x_*, y_*) is an **α-limit point** of (x_0, y_0) if there exists a sequence $t_k \to -\infty$ such that

$$\lim_{k \to \infty} (x(t_k), y(t_k)) = (x_*, y_*).$$

The **ω-limit set** of (x_0, y_0) is the set of all of its ω-limit points; the **α-limit set** of (x_0, y_0) is the set of all of its α-limit points. We denote these sets by $\omega(x_0, y_0)$ and $\alpha(x_0, y_0)$ for brevity. Thus, $\omega(x_0, y_0)$ is the set of all of the accumulation points of the trajectory starting from (x_0, y_0) as t increases – it describes the "future" of the trajectory. The α-limit set describes the "past".

Definition 5.1.2. Let us say that a point (x_0, y_0) is a **periodic** point of the system (5.1.1) if it is not an equilibrium point, and there exists $T > 0$ such that the following holds. Let $(x(t), y(t))$ be the trajectory passing through (x_0, y_0) so that $x(t_0) = x_0$ and $y(t_0) = y_0$. Then

$$x(t_0 + T) = x_0 \text{ and } y(t_0 + T) = y_0.$$

We will say that the point (x_0, y_0) *returns* after time T. The **period** of (x_0, y_0) is the smallest such value of T.

We will say that the trajectory passing through (x_0, y_0) is a **periodic trajectory**.

Thus, a periodic trajectory is a loop. As an example, look at the trajectories of a linear system with a center at the origin (Figure 20, (f)) – each trajectory is periodic except for the equilibrium point at $(0,0)$. The following is a good exercise:

Proposition 5.1.1. *The the period is the same for every point in a periodic trajectory.*

The proof of Proposition 5.1.1 is quite simple. Suppose a pair of functions $\hat{x}(t), \hat{y}(t)$ is a solution of the system (5.1.1), such that the trajectory $(\hat{x}(t), \hat{y}(t))$ is periodic. Let (x_0, y_0) be a point of this trajectory, given by

$$x_0 = \hat{x}(t_0), \ y_0 = \hat{y}(t_0),$$

and suppose that it returns after time $T > 0$. Define a pair of functions

$$u(t) = \hat{x}(t + T) \text{ and } v(t) = \hat{y}(t + T).$$

The pair $(u(t), v(t))$ is a solution of the system (5.1.1) as well (as we have already seen). It also shares an initial condition with $(\hat{x}(t), \hat{y}(t))$:

$$u(t_0) = \hat{x}(t_0 + T) = \hat{x}(t_0) \text{ and } v(t_0) = \hat{y}(t_0 + T) = \hat{y}(t_0).$$

The uniqueness part of the Existence and Uniqueness Theorem tells us that

$$u(t) \equiv \hat{x}(t) \text{ and } v(t) \equiv \hat{y}(t).$$

Now let $(x_1 = \hat{x}(t_1), y_1 = \hat{y}(t_1))$ be any other point of the trajectory. Then

$$x_1 = \hat{x}(t_1) = u(t_1) = \hat{x}(t_1 + T) \text{ and } y_1 = \hat{y}(t_1) = v(t_1) = \hat{y}(t_1 + T).$$

So if one point of a periodic trajectory returns after time T then so does every other point of the trajectory. This implies that all of them have the same period.

Definition 5.1.3. A trajectory $(x(t), y(t))$ is **forward bounded** if there exists $B > 0$ such that

$$|x(t)| < B, \ |y(t)| < B \text{ for all } t \geq 0.$$

A trajectory $(x(t), y(t))$ is **backward bounded** if there exists $B > 0$ such that

$$|x(t)| < B, \ |y(t)| < B \text{ for all } t \leq 0.$$

The following theorem is fundamental in the study of $2D$ systems. It plays the same role as Theorem 3.2.1 does in one dimension, but is, naturally, harder to prove. It is named after Henri Poincaré, who had originally formulated it, and Ivar Bendixson, who had supplied the complete proof. Poincaré (1854-1912) was a mathematical genius. Among his many achievements is the discovery of the Theory of Chaos – which he made by a dramatic "accident" while trying to win a prize established by the King of Sweden for a mathematical description of the dynamics of the Solar system. In brief, Poincaré published a manuscript in a mathematical journal, won the prize for it, found an error in his manuscript, withdrew it and had the journal print a new version, which cost him more than the prize money. In fixing the error, he described a completely new phenomenon which is now known as chaotic dynamics. But I digress. Without further ado, let me formulate the theorem:

Theorem 5.1.1 (Poincaré-Bendixson Theorem). *Suppose $(x(t), y(t))$ is a forward bounded trajectory of a two-dimensional system (5.1.1) passing through (x_0, y_0). Then one of the following possibilities holds:*
(1) $\omega(x_0, y_0)$ contains an equilibrium point;
(2) (x_0, y_0) is a periodic point (so $(x(t), y(t))$ is a periodic trajectory);
(3) $(x(t), y(t))$ is not periodic and $\omega(x_0, y_0)$ is a periodic trajectory.

In case (1) of the theorem, $\omega(x_0, y_0)$ is either a single equilibrium point, or a finite collection of equilibrium points together with separatrices connecting them.

A periodic trajectory which is an ω-limit set of a non-periodic trajectory (as in case (3) of the theorem) is known as a **limit cycle**. We will soon see a very instructive application of limit cycles in a biological model. The moral of Poincaré-Bendixson Theorem is that the behavior of solutions of a two-dimensional system is very regular. It is not quite as simple as in the one-dimensional case (Theorem 3.2.1), which is completely described by the equilibrium points. But the only new kind of behaviour that appears in two-dimension is a periodic oscillation. Two-dimensional systems are widely used for modeling for this reason. The situation changes drastically in dimensions 3 and higher, where chaos reigns.

5.1.2. Good and bad news about limit cycles. Finding equilibrium points of (5.1.1) is completely straightforward: we just need to equate the right-hand sides of the two equations to zero, and solve for x and y. But how does one find a limit cycle?

A good news is that the proof of Poincaré-Bendixson Theorem suggests a recipe for doing it, which I am going to describe now. But a few definitions will be needed first. The first definition is completely straightforward:

Definition 5.1.4. A set $S \subset \mathbb{R}^2$ is **forward invariant** for the system (5.1.1) if for each $(x_0, y_0) \in S$, denoting $(x(t), y(t))$ the trajectory starting at (x_0, y_0) (so that $x(0) = x_0$, $y(0) = y_0$), we have

$$(x(t), y(t)) \in S \text{ for all } t > 0.$$

In other words, a trajectory that starts in S will remain in S for all future time.

If we were to plot the slope field around S, then all of the arrows would point into S, corraling the trajectories into remaining there.

The second definition we will require is that of a closed set in the plane. It is analogous to the definition of a closed interval $[a, b]$ on the real line, which must contain its boundary points a and b. Imagine encircling a region with a pencil on a sheet of paper. The boundary then is the trace of the pencil – it separates the inside of the region from the outside. Here is a formal definition:

Definition 5.1.5. The boundary of a set $S \subset \mathbb{R}^n$ is the set of points $X \in \mathbb{R}^n$ with the following property. For every $r > 0$, the ball of raidus r centered at X contains both points in S and in its complement $\mathbb{R}^n \setminus S$.

We will denote the boundary of S by ∂S (yes, I know, it is the same notation as for a partial derivative – but it is the standard in the literature). A set S is **closed** if it contains its boundary:

$$S \supset \partial S.$$

Here comes the recipe for finding periodic trajectories:

> **Theorem 5.1.2.** *Suppose $S \subset \mathbb{R}^2$ is a closed set which is forward invariant for the system (5.1.1) which does not contain any equilibrium points. Then for every $(x_0, y_0) \in S$ its ω-limit set is a periodic trajectory.*

A closed forward-invariant set is known as a **trapping region** – the orbits are trapped once they enter there. A quick note: the reason we need the set S to be closed in Theorem 5.1.2 is since the periodic orbit may lie on its boundary.

Okay, now for the bad news: there is no guarantee that even when $f(x,y)$ and $g(x,y)$ are very simple functions, we would be able to find trapping regions for all of the limit cycles of the system (5.1.1). In fact, this is a mathematical problem with a famous history. In the year 1900, an illustrious German mathematician David Hilbert presented 23 mathematical problems "of the new 20-th century" at the International Congress of Mathematicians. One of them – the 16th problem – has a question of finding (or at least finding the exact number) of the limit cycles in the case when f and g are both polynomials of degree n.

In 1991/92 Yu. Ilyashenko and J. Écalle showed that every such polynomial system has a finite number of limit cycles (until then even that was not known!) But it is still not known if there is a bound on the number of limit cycles for a given n – it is not even known when f and g are quadratic. On the other hand, as of the present writing no quadratic examples with more than *four* limit cycles are known.

In summary, finding limit cycles is a difficult mathematical problem, and a serious modeling challenge.

5.1.3. An example of finding a trapping region for a limit cycle. Just to give you some idea of how Theorem 5.1.2 can be applied, let us construct an example. It is motivated by a simple model from Newtonian physics: a linear oscillator. Think of a body with mass m, attached to a spring, which obeys the Hooke's Law:

$$F = -kx,$$

where x is the displacement of the spring, and F is the force produced by the spring. By Newton's Law,

$$F = ma = mx'',$$

so putting everything together we get

$$x'' = -\frac{k}{m}x.$$

For simplicity of notation, let us assume $k/m = 1$, and let us also write it as a system in terms of x and $y = x'$ (so that y is the velocity of the body):

(5.1.2)
$$\begin{cases} x' = y \\ y' = -x \end{cases}$$

It is easy to see that the point $(0,0)$ is a center, so every trajectory $(x(t), y(t))$ of this system will be periodic. In fact, all trajectories are circles in the xy-plane centered at the origin. One clever way to see this is as follows. Let us denote

$$D(x,y) = x^2 + y^2$$

the square of the distance to the origin. Then, by the Chain Rule,

$$\frac{d}{dt}D(x(t), y(t)) = 2x(t)\frac{d}{dt}x(t) + 2y(t)\frac{d}{dt}y(t),$$

and substituting the right-hand sides of the equations (5.1.2), we further see that

$$\frac{d}{dt}D(x(t), y(t)) = 2x(t)y(t) - 2y(t)x(t) = 0,$$

and thus every point of a trajectory lies at the same distance from the origin.

To make the model slightly more realistic, we can add the force of friction, which will be negatively proportional to the velocity (that is, it will "slow down" the motion):

(5.1.3)
$$\begin{cases} x' = y \\ y' = -x - cy \end{cases}$$

where $c > 0$. Repeating the same calculation for a trajectory of (5.1.3), we get

$$\frac{d}{dt}D(x(t), y(t)) = 2x(t)y(t) - 2y(t)(x(t) + cy(t)) = -c(y(t))^2 \le 0,$$

so the distance to the origin will decrease. Indeed, the origin is a stable spiral point here.

Finally, let us modify the system by replacing the friction term $-cy$ in the system (5.1.3) with a non-linear term

$$-cy(x^2 + 2y^2 - 1),$$

transforming it into

(5.1.4)
$$\begin{cases} x' = y \\ y' = -x - cy(x^2 + 2y^2 - 1) \end{cases}$$

Such models are sometimes known as *self-excited oscillators*. When x and y are small, the non-linear term turns positive and becomes "anti-friction" of sorts, adding energy to the system rather than dissipating it. More precisely, along a trajectory of (5.1.4) we have

$$\frac{d}{dt}D(x(t),y(t)) = 2x(t)y(t) - 2y(t)(x(t) + c((x(t))^2 + 2(y(t))^2 - 1).$$

Note that if $D(x,y) = 4$, then

$$(x(t))^2 + 2(y(t))^2 \geq (x(t))^2 + (y(t))^2 = 4 > 1,$$

so the expression $\frac{d}{dt}D(x(t),y(t))$ will be *negative* along the circle of radius two around the origin. All trajectories crossing this circle will point inwards of it. Similarly, if $D(x,y) = \frac{1}{4}$, then

$$(x(t))^2 + 2(y(t))^2 \leq 2(x(t))^2 + 2(y(t))^2 = \frac{1}{2} < 1,$$

so $\frac{d}{dt}D(x(t),y(t)) \geq 0$ along the circle of radius $1/2$ around the origin. All trajectories crossing this circle will point outwards. Finally, the system (5.1.4), just like the previous two, has a single equilibrium point $(0,0)$. This means that the annulus

$$A = \{(x,y) \mid \frac{1}{4} \leq D(x,y) \leq 4\}$$

is a trapping region, and Theorem 5.1.2 implies that the ω-limit set of any point in A is a periodic trajectory in A. In fact, there is a unique such trajectory, which is the limit cycle attracting every other trajectory in A (see Figure 27).

5.2. Interlude: the curse of dimensionality

As we saw in the previous chapter, a nonlinear model which is described by a single coordinate (or degree of freedom as physicists sometime say) $x(t)$ is easily predictable. Theorem 3.2.1 gives a complete summary of possible scenarios for a trajectory $x(t)$ as well as a recipe for identifying them starting with an initial condition $x(t_0) = x_0$. Visualization of a one-dimensional phase diagram is equally easy and straightforward.

A model with two degrees of freedom $x(t)$ and $y(t)$ requires a much more in-depth analysis. Poincaré-Bendixson Theorem does tell us what future scenarios are possible for the behaviour of the model. Identifying which one of them applies to a trajectory starting at $x(t_0) = x_0, y(t_0) = y_0$ is challenging at best, as only partial recipes exist. Visualization of the trajectories via a phase portrait is a very helpful tool, but putting one together

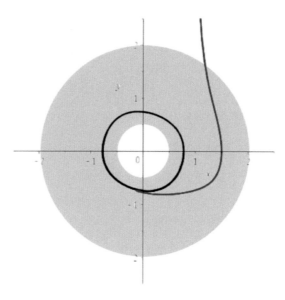

Figure 27. The limit cycle for the system (5.1.4). The trapping region A is in gray, a sample trajectory which enters A is shown in blue.

is difficult – even when limit cycles are absent (or at least we believe that they are absent) from the picture.

There is no analogue of Theorem 3.2.1 or Poincaré-Bendixson Theorem in dimension 3. The behaviour of three dimensional models may be too complex, and too unstable with respect to the initial values (the phenomenon known informally as Chaos) to give any deterministic predictions. Sophisticated methods of statistical sampling are sometimes used for such models with varying degree of success. In any case, a complete understanding of possible behaviours of 3D models is lacking. Trajectories can still be visualized in 3D, it is not as easy as in 2D, of course, but at least it is possible. Beyond three dimensions, even this is no longer doable, so a model may become completely intractable.

This rapid climb in complexity from low-dimensional models to higher-dimensional ones is known as "the curse of dimensionality". It is common both in modeling and in analyzing data, and the aim of most of analytics is to distill the few principal degrees of freedom in the data so that it becomes tractable. A common temptation when designing a mathematical model of a complex biological process is to equip it with many parameters which are supposed to better describe the complexity of the real world. This is generally counterproductive – the more dimensions we add the less sense the modeling will make. It is no accident that the models we have considered so far, and will consider in the next chapter, are very low-dimensional. In a way, that is their greatest strength.

5.3. Modeling the human heartbeat

The heart is a pump which expands and contracts cyclically to circulate blood through the body. The extreme relaxed state of the heart is called the *diastole*. The cycle of a heartbeat starts when the heart is in the diastolic state. At this point of the cycle, the heart muscle fibers are at their longest. The *pacemaker* in the heart triggers an electrochemical wave that slowly spreads. This electrochemical wave causes the muscle fibers to contract, first slowly, pushing the blood into the lower chambers of the heart, and then rapidly. The rapid contraction sends the heart into the extreme contracted state, known as the *systole*. This forces the blood into the lungs and the arteries. Immediately following the systolic state, the heart muscles start to relax again, returning the heart to the dyastolic state and completing a single heartbeat.

In 1972, E. Zeeman **[Ze72]** proposed a simple yet ingenious mathematical model of the heartbeat. It has two important features:

- a stable limit cycle of the heartbeat;
- a threshold for triggering the pacemaker to go into the systolic state.

Here is the somewhat simplified model:

(5.3.1)
$$\begin{cases} x' = y \\ y' = A(-x + Ty - y^3) \end{cases}$$

where A and T are some parameters of the model. Let us explain the meaning of the unknowns. The variable y is the length of the muscle fiber, with $y = 0$ corresponding to the midpoint between the diastole and the systole (thus, y is negative in the systole, and positive in the diastole). The variable x is the electric signal of the pacemaker in the heart. To fix the ideas, let us quite arbitrarily fix $A = 1$ and $T = 3$, so the system (5.3.1) becomes

(5.3.2)
$$\begin{cases} x' = y \\ y' = -x + 3y - y^3 \end{cases}$$

Firstly, let us note that the system has only one equilibrium point $(0,0)$.

Figure 28. The cubic is the y-nullcline of the system (5.3.2). The arrows indicate the direction of the slope field. The dotted lines bound the trapping region for the limit cycle of the heartbeat.

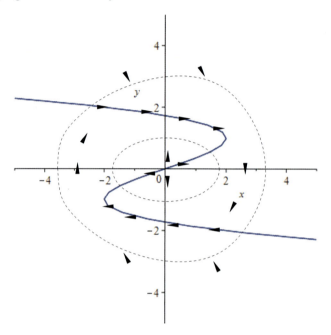

The x-nullcline is the x-axis, and the y-nullcline is the graph of the cubic function $x = 3y - y^3$ (see Figure 28). The arrows of the slope field are horizontal on the graph of the cubic, leading right above the x-axis, and left below the x-axis. The arrows are tilted up below the cubic, and up above it.

The inspection of the arrows of the slope field in the figure suggests that $(0,0)$ is a repelling point. That is correct – but you should verify it for yourself, using linearization. To understand what the picture is telling us, let us try to understand a trajectory which starts just above the graph of the cubic, around $x = -3$. The slope field is almost horizontal near the graph, and the graph itself is almost horizontal. So the trajectory will slide to the right essentially along the curve of the graph. This happens practically without the change of the length of the heart muscle, until we run out of the nearly horizontal portion of the cubic graph. Just as the trajectory moves past $x = 2$, it will "fall off the cliff", leaving the graph of the cubic behind. The arrows will turn down, and the further we get away from the y-nullcline, the sharper will be the downward slope, accelerating the contraction of the heart. This is the threshold effect – as the pacemaker's signal reaches a certain value, the muscle will contract sharply.

Continuing down, we will encounter the cubic again, and crossing it will find ourselves in a situation which mirrors the start of the cycle. Now the arrows are again parallel to the cubic, leading us nearly horizontally left – until the pacemaker's electrochemical wave dissipates and the arrows take us sharply up, relaxing the heart and completing the cycle. It is not difficult to draw a trapping region in this picture – look at the dotted lines. The outer contour traps the trajectories, and the inner one cuts out the equilibrium $(0,0)$ to satisfy the conditions of Theorem 5.1.2 (this is possible since the slope field points away from the repelling equilibrium point).

Theorem 5.1.2 guarantees the existence of a limit cycle, which is depicted in Figure 29. The systole is near $(3, -2)$ and the diastole is around $(-3, 2)$.

Figure 29. The limit cycle of the system (5.3.2) The arrows of the slope field are also shown, together with the y-nullcline.

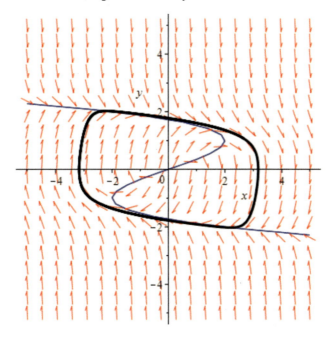

5.4. Oscillating chemical reactions

5.4.1. A "supposedly discovered discovery". In 1951 a Russian chemist Boris Belousov was trying to imitate the so-called "Krebs cycle", which is a series of chemical reactions used by cells of aerobic organisms to release stored energy. Mixing several chemicals in a test tube he observed something astonishing – the solution started to change color repeatedly (from yellow to colorless and back), oscillating for close to an hour. In Belousov's day, it was believed that the concentrations of the products of a chemical reaction must approach an equilibrium rapidly and monotonically. This was obviously not the case in Belousov's finding, where the changing colors indicated that the concentrations of the products of the reaction were *oscillating with time* instead of settling down.

As scientists joke sarcastically, "never let experimental facts get in the way of a good theory". This is precisely what the editors of the journals to which Belousov tried submitting his paper did, rejecting it repeatedly. Reportedly, one of them added a nasty remark about a "supposedly discovered discovery" to the rejection letter.

Ten years later, a Russian graduate student Anatol Zhabotinsky was directed by his advisor to look into Belousov's reaction – a risky career move for a young scientist! Zhabotinsky investigated the reaction in detail and confirmed Belousov's findings, developing a theoretical model for it. He presented the findings at an international conference in Prague in 1968, bringing a belated acclaim to Belousov's discovery. The reaction is now known as Belousov-Zhabotinsky (or simply BZ) reaction, and numerous other oscillating reactions have been discovered since. In the next section, we will discuss one of them, known as Lengyel-Epstein reaction [**LeEp91**]. It is less involved than the BZ reaction and admits a simpler mathematical model.

5.4.2. An example of an oscillating reaction. In the example we will look at, there are two reactants whose concentrations oscillate with time. Denoting these concentrations $x(t), y(t)$, the authors of [**LeEp91**] suggested

the following mathematical model, describing the rates at which these concentrations change:

(5.4.1)
$$\begin{cases} x' = a - x - \dfrac{4xy}{1+x^2} \\ y' = bx\left(1 - \dfrac{y}{1+x^2}\right) \end{cases}$$

where a and b are some positive parameters.

Differential equations and rate laws in chemistry. Why would a chemical reaction be described by *differential equations*? Indeed, from basic Chemistry we learn at school (my apologies to any present or future Chemists reading this), we expect a reaction to be captured by a formula which shows the reactants on one side and the products of the reaction on the other; something like this example

$$A + B \longrightarrow C + D,$$

in which two particles (molecules, atoms, ions) A and B combined produce a C particle and a D particle. Kinetic Chemistry asks at what rate the reaction proceeds, or, in other words, at what rate C (or D) is produced. In the simplest scenario, particles of A and B would randomly bump into each other in the test tube to react. The rate at which this would happen would be proportional to the product of their numbers in the test tube volume, that is, of their concentrations. If we denote $[P]$ the concentration of P, then we will arrive to an equation of the form

$$\frac{d[C]}{dt} = k[A][B],$$

saying that the rate of production of C in a unit of volume is proportional to the product of the concentrations of A and B. Here the coefficient k may depend on things like temperature (which makes particle "bounce around" the test tube more, and thus more likely to meet), presence of catalysts, and so on. Look at the reaction described by

$$2A + B \longrightarrow 3A + D.$$

Here, two particles of A have to meet at the same time, so the rate of production of A on the right will be proportional to the likelyhood of A meeting another A and B at the same time – which gives

$$\frac{d[A]}{dt} = k[A]^2[B]$$

(to convince yourself of this, give A an alias, say W, and re-write the reaction as $W + A + B \longrightarrow 3A + D$.)

Such *rate laws* which correspond to *elementary reactions* are easy to deduce from the chemical formulas. However, a typical reaction may involve many elementary steps, intertwined in ways that are difficult to understand. Rate laws for such reactions are usually deduced experimentally. They will still be expressed via differential equations, which involve combinations of (not necessarily integer) powers of the variables. The system (5.4.1) is an example of such an empirical rate law.

At first sight, the system (5.4.1) may appear intimidating, but let us be brave and attempt to analyze it. Firstly, x and y are concentrations of chemicals, and therefore, both are positive. The equilibrium points of the system are given by

(5.4.2)
$$\begin{cases} f(x,y) = a - x - \dfrac{4xy}{1+x^2} = 0 \\ g(x,y) = bx \left(1 - \dfrac{y}{1+x^2} \right) = 0 \end{cases}$$

The second equation gives
$$y = 1 + x^2,$$

and if we plug this into the first equation, we will obtain
$$a - 5x = 0, \text{ or } x = a/5,$$

so that
$$y = 1 + (a/5)^2.$$

Thus, there is a single equilibrium point
$$x_* = a/5, \ y_* = 1 + x_*^2 = 1 + (a/5)^2.$$

Calculating the Jacobian at this point is a little messy, but not overly complicated. For instance,
$$\frac{\partial f}{\partial x}(x,y) = -1 - \frac{4y(1+x^2) - 8x^2 y}{(1+x^2)^2} = \frac{-(1+x^2)^2 - 4y(1+x^2) + 8x^2 y}{(1+x^2)^2}.$$

Replacing $1 + x_*^2$ with y_*, we get
$$\frac{\partial f}{\partial x}(x_*,y_*) = \frac{-5y_* + 8x_*^2}{y_*} = \frac{-5 + 3x_*^2}{y_*}.$$

Proceeding with the other partial derivatives, we end up with
$$\text{Jac}_{x_*,y_*} = \begin{pmatrix} \dfrac{3x_*^2 - 5}{y_*} & \dfrac{-4x_*}{y_*} \\ \dfrac{2bx_*^2}{y_*} & \dfrac{-bx_*}{y_*} \end{pmatrix}$$

The determinant of this matrix is

$$\Delta = \frac{5bx_*^3 + 5bx_*}{y_*^2} = \frac{5bx_*}{y_*} > 0.$$

The trace is

$$\tau = \frac{3x_*^2 - 5 - bx_*}{y_*} = \frac{\frac{a}{5}\left(\frac{3a}{5} - \frac{25}{a} - b\right)}{y_*}.$$

We thus see that (x_*, y_*) is a repelling equilibrium point if

$$\tau > 0, \text{ or } b < b_c \equiv \frac{3a}{5} - \frac{25}{a}.$$

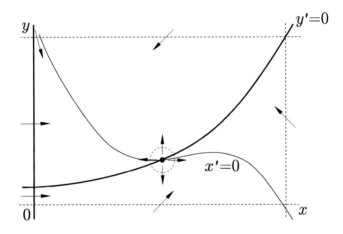

Figure 30. A trapping region for the system (5.4.1) for $b < b_c$ is the rectangle in the figure with a disk around the equilibrium point removed. The x-nullcline is indicated by a thin solid line, the y-nullclines are marked by thick solid lines.

In Figure 30, we see the x and y nullclines of the system (5.4.1), not quite drawn to scale to make room for the arrows. Note that the rectangle bounded by the dotted lines and the y-axis is forward invariant. If $b < b_c$, then the equilibrium point is repelling, so if we remove a small disk around (x_*, y_*) from the rectangle, as shown in the figure, then the resulting region is forward invariant, closed, and does not contain any fixed points. By Poincaré-Bendixson Theorem, every trajectory in this region converges to a limit cycle. In fact, there is a single limit cycle here, responsible for the oscillations of values of $x(t)$ and $y(t)$ in this chemical reaction. In Figure 31 we see how a trajectory starting at $x(0) = 1$, $y(0) = 1$ converges to this limit cycle for the values $a = 10$, $b = 2$.

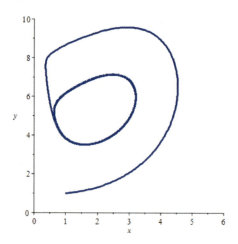

Figure 31. The trajectory starting at $(1,1)$ rapidly converges to the limit cycle for the system (5.4.1) with $a = 10$, $b = 2 < b_c$.

1. As we have seen, it typically takes some work to prove that a 2D system has a limit cycle. Let us use a bit of cheating to make up an example in which it is easy to do. Consider the following system of differential equations written in *polar coordinates* (r, θ):

$$\begin{cases} \dfrac{dr}{dt} = r(1 - r^2) \\ \dfrac{d\theta}{dt} = 1 \end{cases}$$

The same system can be (via some mildly unpleasant algebraic manipulations) written in the standard (x, y) coordinates as

$$\begin{cases} \dfrac{dx}{dt} = x(1 - x^2 - y^2) - y \\ \dfrac{dy}{dt} = x + y(1 - x^2 - y^2) \end{cases}$$

However, the polar form is much easier to analyze, since r and θ are described by two unconnected differential equations:

(a) Draw a *one-dimensional* phase diagram for $r(t)$.

(b) Use the phase diagram from part (a) to identify all equilibrium points and periodic trajectories of the system. What is the stability of the equilibrium points? Are there any limit cycles?

(c) Sketch the phase portrait.

2. Design a 2D system in polar coordinates which has exactly two limit cycles.

3. ☺ Prove that there does not exist a two-dimensional phase portrait with exactly one limit cycle, and no other periodic trajectories or equilibrium points.

4. ☺ **A more complicated (and realistic) predator-prey problem.** Consider a predator-prey problem with type II functional response by the

predators to the number of prey (compare with Problem 6 in the exercises for Chapter 3):

(5.4.3)
$$\begin{cases} x' = x \left(1 - x - \dfrac{2y}{1 + 2x} \right) \\ y' = y \left(-\dfrac{1}{6} + \dfrac{2x}{1 + 2x} \right) \end{cases}$$

(a) Verify that there are three equilibrium points with $x \geq 0$, $y \geq 0$. Find them, and classify them by their type and stability. Show that there is only one equilibrium point inside the first quadrant, and this point is repelling.

(b) Consider the function $F(x,y) = x + y$, and verify that
$$\frac{d}{dt} F(x(t), y(t)) < 0 \text{ on the line } F(x,y) = 6.$$

(c) Conclude that there is a trapping region for a limit cycle, and use a computer algebra system to plot the limit cycle.

As a side note to this exercise, let me mention that cyclical fluctuations are typical in real-life predator-prey ecosystems. A favorite example from the literature is given by fluctuations in the population of Canada lynx and snowshoe hare the lynx predates on. The data goes back to early-1800's, and is based on the number of pelts of lynx and hare purchased by the Hudson's Bay Company (see Figure 32). It clearly shows a 10-year oscillation in the number of pelts for both species, consistent with periodic oscillations in the sizes of the populations.

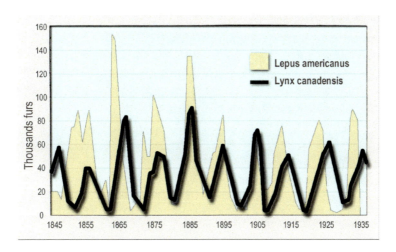

Figure 32. Oscillations in the number of furs bought by the Hudson's Bay Company for Canada lynx (*Lynx canadensis*) and snowshoe hare (*Lepus americanus*). Source: *Wikipedia,* by Lamiot.

References for Chapter 5

[LeEp91]   I. Lengyel, I.R. Epstein, *Modeling of Turing structures in the chlorite-iodide-malonic acid-starch reaction.* Science, **251**(1991), 650

[Ze72]   E.C. Zeeman, *Differential equations for the heartbeat and nerve impulse.* In: Waddington, C.H. (Ed.), *Towards a Theoretical Biology* 4: Essays, 8–67, Edinburgh University Press; 1972

A hot topic: epidemiological modeling

6.1. Compartmentalized epidemic models

6.1.1. Yes, SIR!. The models of this type were first described by Kermack and McKendrick in 1927 [**KeMcK27**] and have become the basis for most of the epidemiological literature since. Let us start with the best-known of them, called the SIR (Susceptible-Infected-Recovered) model. In this model, as in all other compartmentalized models, the population is divided into *compartments*, or *bins*, according to their status with respect to the infection (see Figure 33 for an illustration): *Susceptible* or not immune, *Infected* and infectious, and *Recovered* and immune. We denote the size of each of the three sub-populations by its first letter: $S(t)$, $I(t)$, $R(t)$. The total population is then

$$(6.1.1) \qquad N = S + I + R.$$

The model will be based on several assumptions. The first one is:

Assumption I: the birth rate in the population is equal to the death rate, and the death rate in each of the bins is the same.

First, why this assumption is useful. It implies that the size of the population N in (6.1.1) is constant. This is priceless in the analysis of the model, because it allows one to replace a three-dimensional system of equations (for S, I, and R variables) with a two-dimensional one, since we can use (6.1.1) to express any of the three variables through the other two. There are obvious limitations of the assumption. To begin with, it does not apply to diseases with a high mortality rate – the death rate in bin I would then be considerably higher than in the other two. It also limits the time span of the model, since over a long period of time the value of N may change significantly – but this seems quite reasonable if the time span of the epidemic is measured in months, not in decades.

Figure 33. An illustration of the SIR model

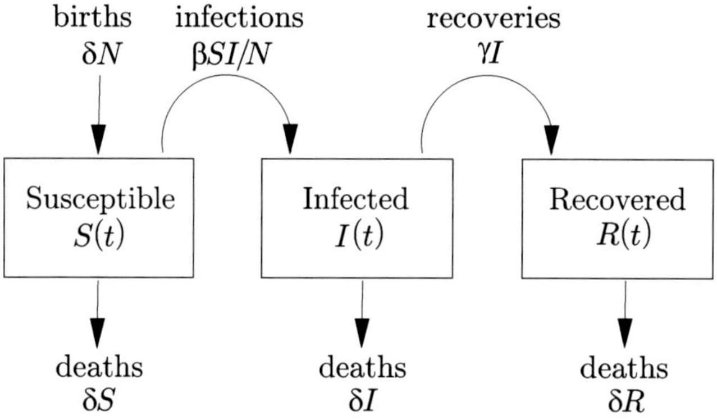

Assumption II: the immunity is permanent – so R(ecovered) become immune and cannot be reinfected.

This is obviously true for some diseases, such as measles, for instance. Emphatically not true for others, such as many STDs. Somewhat untrue for ilnesses such as various strains of the flu – for which immunity may vane with time or as the pathogen mutates.

Now for the good stuff. The key to the model is the rate at which the susceptible individuals become infected.

Assumption III: the whole population mixes at random, so that each individual member of the population has an equal chance of coming in contact with every other individual.

This assumption means that the rate of infection is proportional to the fraction of the infected individuals in the society (since we have an equal chance of coming in contact with either an infected individual or a non-infected one as the population is randomly mixed):

$$\text{rate of infection} = \beta\frac{I}{N},$$

where β reflects the ease of transmitting the specific infection.

This assumption is the most questionable, and, in fact, has been questioned repeatedly in the literature. There are scenarios under which it seems reasonable (a classroom, a cruiseship, a military base). On the other hand, I am writing this sentence in Toronto, which at present has a population of around 3 million people. How often do I mix with most of them? Obviously, never. But there is a small group of them with whom I mix all the time. How much does incorporating this assumption weakens the usability of the model? It is not easy to say, but we will try to shed some light on that as well as discuss some alternatives shortly.

With the above three assumptions, we can produce the equations of the model. Let us start with the equation for $S'(t)$. There is a positive contribution here, coming from the birth rate. Everyone is born susceptible (well, this is really another assumption, but so be it), so we increment $S'(t)$ by $\delta N = \delta(S + I + R)$ where $\delta =$ birth rate. The death rate is also δ, so we lose δS. The infection rate is $\beta I/N$, so we decrease $S'(t)$ by $(\beta I/N) \cdot S$. The end result is the equation

$$(6.1.2) \qquad S' = \delta(S + I + R) - \delta S - \beta\frac{IS}{N} = \delta(I + R) - \beta\frac{IS}{N}.$$

The infected susceptibles go into the I bin, so the next equation is

$$(6.1.3) \qquad I' = -\delta I + \beta\frac{IS}{N} - \gamma I,$$

where γ is the rate at which infected members of the population recover. Finally,

$$(6.1.4) \qquad R' = -\delta R + \gamma I.$$

We get three equations, but formula (6.1.1) lets us to get rid of one of them. For instance, we can express

$$R = N - I - S,$$

which then gives us the system

$$(6.1.5) \qquad \textbf{SIR model} \quad \begin{cases} S' = \delta(N - S) - \beta\frac{IS}{N} \\ \\ I' = -(\delta + \gamma)I + \beta\frac{IS}{N} \end{cases}$$

It is easy to change the "rules of the game" by adding or subtracting more bins as needed. For instance, there could be an incubation period during which infected individuals cannot transmit the disease. That would add one more bin to the model. On the other hand, recovered individuals may have no immunity. In that case, the R bin simply disappears, as recoveries go back into the S bin. The model then becomes

$$(6.1.6) \qquad \textbf{SIS model} \quad \begin{cases} S' = \delta(N - S) + \gamma I - \beta\frac{IS}{N} \\ \\ I' = -(\delta + \gamma)I + \beta\frac{IS}{N} \end{cases}$$

A SIS model is particularly easy to analyze, since with only two bins in the model one has

$$S + I = N.$$

Substituting $S = N - I$ into the second equation, we get (after a bit of algebraic manipulation):

$$(6.1.7) \qquad I' = \frac{\beta}{N}I\left(N\left(1 - \frac{\delta + \gamma}{\beta}\right) - I\right).$$

This is our old friend, the logistic equation. There is one equilibrium point that would inevitably be present in all of these models: $I = 0$ (so $S = N$) which corresponds to the absence of any infections. Setting the parentheses equal to zero, we will obtain a second equilibrium point

$$I_* = N\left(1 - \frac{\delta + \gamma}{\beta}\right).$$

We are only interested in the case $I_* > 0$ which corresponds to

$$\frac{\delta + \gamma}{\beta} < 1 \text{ or } R_0 \equiv \frac{\beta}{\delta + \gamma} > 1.$$

This is the *endemic equilibrium* of the model, when the infection does not disappear from the population. The quantity R_0 ("R-naught"), called the *basic reproductive number*, has gained a semi-mystical significance in popular culture.

At the initial stage, when I is small, we can neglect it in the parentheses, and obtain an approximately constant per capita growth rate of the infected population

$$\frac{I'}{I} = \frac{\beta}{N}\left(N\left(1 - \frac{\delta + \gamma}{\beta}\right) - I\right) \approx \beta - (\gamma + \delta),$$

yielding a nearly exponential rate of increase when $\beta > \gamma + \delta$. Since $\gamma + \delta$ indicates the proportion of the number of infected people either recovering or dying *per unit of time*, its reciprocal,

$$T_i = \frac{1}{\gamma + \delta}$$

can be interpreted as the length of time an infected person may remain infectious (do a quick mental experiment to convince yourself of this – ignore the deaths, and imagine that $1/10$-th of all infected people recover in a day; then it would take 10 days to clear all of the infections). Assuming that I' stays roughly constant over the average infectious period of time T_i we see that the increment of the value of I over this period is

$$\Delta I \approx I' T_i.$$

Combining this with the previous estimate, we see that at the early stage of the epidemic, the model predicts that

$$\Delta I \approx \left(\frac{\beta}{\gamma + \delta} - 1\right) I = R_0 I - I.$$

The right-hand side of the formula represents the I new recoveries (if we start with I infected people, all of them should recover over the period T_i which corresponds to the term $-I$) and $R_0 I$ new infections. In other words, at the start of the epidemic, I infected people will produce $R_0 I$ new infections over the period of time they remain infectious, or, simply put, *one infected person will infect R_0 people on average*. This is the usual interpretation of R_0 in compartmental models. Of course, the per capita growth rate of the number of infected people cannot be constant, since $I(t)$ has to level off with time, so this only applies to the early stages. Epidemiologists talk about estimating R_t, which is the number of people an average infected person will spread the infection to after time t has passed from the start of the epidemic.

A word of caution is in order here. Even within the confines of the compartmental models, estimating R_0 or R_t in real time is challenging at best, since the models are non-linear, and there are many unknown quantities involved in estimating the rate of growth of infections in a population. I recommend a nicely written survey [**Rid14**] which highlights these challenges, and discusses how early estimates of R_0 led to mistaken assumptions in the H1N1 flu epidemic of 2009. A more recent illustration of this is the paper [**Lour20**] which appeared in March 2020, and concerned the epidemic of Covid-19 in the UK. It showed how different, and completely plausible, sets of assumptions about the parameters of a SIR model of the epidemic would lead to dramatically different long-term predictions, but *would all fit* the data available at the time.

Of course, no matter the interpretation of R_0, it is only a feature of the model and has no intrinsic biological significance.

An SIR model is more difficult to study, but the analysis goes along the same lines. Setting the right-hand side of the second equation of (6.1.5) equal to zero, we again find two equilibrium points: the infection-free equilibrium $I = 0$ (and $S = N$), and the endemic equilibrium

$$S_* = N\frac{\delta + \gamma}{\beta} = \frac{N}{R_0}, \text{ and } I_* = \frac{\delta N}{\beta}(R_0 - 1),$$

where once again

$$R_0 = \frac{\beta}{\delta + \gamma}.$$

So if $R_0 < 1$, then the endemic equilibrium does not exist in our model (since a population cannot be negative).

Let us study the stability of the infection-free equilibrium, to see if the disease can disappear from the population completely in this model. With a little bit of algebra we can find the Jacobian of the system at $(S = N, I = 0)$. It is equal to

(6.1.8)
$$\text{Jac}_{N,0} = \begin{bmatrix} -\delta & -\beta \\ 0 & \beta - \delta - \gamma \end{bmatrix}$$

The eigenvalues of this matrix are

$$\lambda_1 = -\delta, \lambda_2 = \beta - (\gamma + \delta).$$

The first one is always negative, and the second one is negative if $\beta < (\gamma + \delta)$ (in other words, if $R_0 < 1$). Thus, if $R_0 < 1$ then the infection-free

equilibrium is attracting, and (at least if the number of infected is sufficiently low) the disease disappears from the population. If $R_0 > 1$, then
$\lambda_2 > 0$ and the infection-free equilibrium is unstable.

Figure 34. An example of an SIR model for a population of size $N = 1000$. The (somewhat unrealistic) values of the parameters are $\delta = 0.1$, $\gamma = 0.2$, $\beta = 0.8$, which yields $R_0 = 8/3 > 1$, and a stable endemic equilibrium $S_* = 375$, $I_* \approx 208.33$. On the left is a graph of $I(t)$ starting with $I(0) = 100$, $S(0) = 900$. We see a "wave" of infections, settling at the endemic equilibrium value $I(t) \xrightarrow[t \to +\infty]{} I_*$. On the right is the phase portrait, showing the epidemic equilibrium attracting the corresponding trajectory.

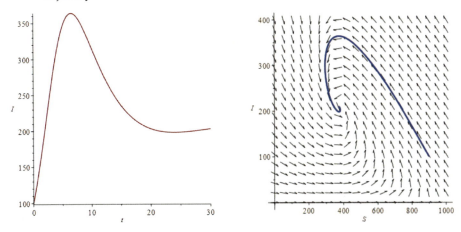

Linearizing the system at the endemic equilibrium (S_*, I_*) we get (verify the calculation):

$$(6.1.9) \qquad \mathrm{Jac}_{S_*,I_*} = \begin{bmatrix} -\delta R_0 & -(\delta+\gamma) \\ \delta(R_0-1) & 0 \end{bmatrix}$$

The trace of this matrix is $\tau = -\delta R_0$ and the determinant is $\Delta = \delta(\delta + \gamma)(R_0 - 1)$. So if $R_0 > 1$, we have $\tau < 0$, $\Delta > 0$, which makes the equilibrium attracting, so the disease does not dissapear and becomes endemic
(see Figure 34).

Maple code for Figure 34 Here is the code I used. I began by defining
the system. I replaced I with L, so that Maple would not confuse it with the
imaginary unit.

```
>with(DEtools):with(plots):
>de1:=diff(S(t),t)=d*(N-S(t))-b*L(t)*S(t)/N;
```

```
>de2:=diff(L(t),t)=-(d+g)*L(t)+b*L(t)*S(t)/N;
```
Next, I specified the parameters. I used Latin letters in lieu of Greek ones.
```
>d:=0.1;g:=0.2;b:=0.8;N:=1000;
```
I solved the system numerically with initial values $S(0) = 900$, $I(0) = 100$ to find the functions $S(t)$ and $I(t)$:
```
>sol:=dsolve([de1,de2,S(0)=900,L(0)=100],numeric,
                        output=listprocedure);
```
And plotted the function $I(t)$:
```
>Lout:=rhs(sol[2]);
>plot(Lout(t),t=0..30);
```
The phase portrait on the right-hand side of the figure is produced by the command:
```
>DEplot({de1,de2},[S(t),L(t)],0..300,{[0,900,100]},S=0..1000,
            L=0..400,color=black,linecolor=blue,stepsize=0.2);
```

It is difficult to overstate the importance of compartmentalized models in theoretical epidemiology. However, their key weakness, which we have already discussed above, is the assumption of the homogeneous mixing of the population, which brings everyone in contact with everyone else with an equal probability. What if we try to restrict the interactions to the circle of friends/neighbors/acquaintances one is actually likely to come in contact with? At the other extreme, this will lead to a model in which each infected member of the population is only able to spread the infection to a handful of others. A good analogy is a spread of wildfire in the forest – from a burning tree to the neighboring trees. In the next section, we will explore this analogy, which will shed a rather different light on the dynamics of an epidemic spread.

6.2. Spreading like wildfire

Comparison of epidemics with wildfires is probably as old as wildfires... or as epidemics. But adopting this comparison suggests a very different approach to modeling than compartmentalization analysis from the previous section. Indeed, the key to the SIR/SIS models and the like is what we called Assumption III – the population mixes uniformly at random, so each individual in the population has an equal and small chance of coming in contact with every other individual. This assumption means that there is no difference between, say, infected individuals – their social contacts matter not since they will be equally likely to infect anyone susceptible – and thus all we need to know is their overall number. In a dramatic contrast, a forest fire spreads from a tree to a neighboring tree – so an infected individual can only infect the "neighbors" in the social network, if we accept this model of spread.

To gain some understanding into this approach to modeling epidemics, let us describe a beautiful and very insightful mathematical model of a forest fire. This class of models is known as **percolation models**. The con-

Figure 35. Percolation on a square grid. Light gray edges are "closed", black edges are "open"

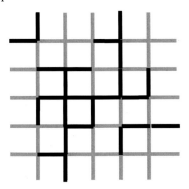

struction is illustrated in Figure 35. Consider a square $N \times N$ grid. For each edge connecting two vertices of the grid let us designate it "open" (black in the figure) with probability $p \in [0, 1]$ or "closed" (gray in the figure) with probability $1 - p$. To understand this better, imagine that you have an unfair coin, which lands heads in $100 \cdot p\%$ of the tosses, and lands tails in $100 \cdot (1 - p)\%$ of the tosses. For each of the edges of the grid, we toss the coin once, and color the edge black if it lands heads, and gray if it lands tails.

The open edges, colored black, are the conduits of transmission of the fire (or the infection, if you prefer). The closed gray ones are not. Of course, the proportion of open edges will very much depend on the value of p. If $p = 1$, then all edges are open, and if p is close to 1 then there will be very few closed edges, so the fire can spread along most of them. On the other hand, if $p = 0$ then there are no open edges at all, and if p is sufficiently close to 0 then most edges will be closed, so the fire would not have much chance of spreading.

To give a concrete meaning to what we call the spreading of the fire, let us say that there is *percolation* in the grid if there is an open path from the bottom side to the top side of the square. The choice of the word is motivated by the image of a liquid slowly seeping through the open channels in the grid and coming out at the other edge. So that will be our measure of the spread of the fire – a presence of percolation means that it can spread all the way across the grid, and its absence means that it must spontaneously stop spreading before reaching the far edge, by running into a wall of gray.

Of course, the higher the value of p, the higher the probability of percolation. We could get exceptionally lucky with our coin tosses, and get a percolation path even if p is close to 0 – but that would be very unlikely if the grid is large. Now here is a question: what should be the choice of p so that the presence of percolation becomes more likely than not? After all, our problem is finite: we have a finite number of $N \times N$ pictures colored gray and black; and the choice of p determines the likelyhood of each of those pictures. And since as p increases from 0 to 1, the likelyhood of having percolation also increases from 0 to 1, there is a number $p_N \in [0, 1]$ after which the global spread of the fire becomes a better bet.

Let us formulate a theorem:

Theorem 6.2.1. *The following properties hold for the percolation model:*

(I) *As $N \to \infty$ we have $p_N \to 0.5$.*

(II) *If $p < 0.5$ then as $N \to \infty$ the probability of having a percolation path converges to zero.*

(III) *If $p > 0.5$ then as $N \to \infty$ the probability of having a percolation path converges to one.*

The statements (II) and (III) imply that, in practice, if we select $p > 0.5$, take a large grid, and color edges black with probability p, then we will *almost always* see a percolation path. On the other hand, if we do the same with $p < 0.5$ then it will almost never happens. This is a manifestation of a probabilistic principle known as Zero-One Law. I will not dwell on it further, and will let the Stats fans among the readers do a literature search of their own.

But I will explain to you why 0.5. Let us do a simple mental exercise

Figure 36. Symmetry in the model. Either a gray percolation path or a black percolation path could exist – but not both!

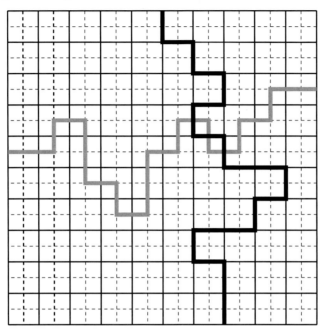

– let us shift all the gray edges half a grid square down, and half a grid square to the left. The black edges will stay in place. Now we will still consider black edges open for percolation from bottom to top. But we will also consider gray edges open for percolation *from left to right* (see Figure 36). Then the following is obvious:

A black up-down path exists if and only if a gray left-right path does not exist, and vice versa.

This symmetry means that

$$p_N \approx 1 - p_N$$

since the two events: a likely appearance of a vertical path, and a likely disappearance of a horizontal path happen at the same time as we increase p. I use an approximate equality sign "$\approx$", rather than true equality, since the two grids are slighlty different (off by a half of a grid square). But as $N \to \infty$ this minor discrepancy matters less and less. In the limit, we obtain the threshold value

$$0.5 = 1 - 0.5.$$

It is known as the **critical probability** and denoted p_c.

Let me point out to you how counterintuitive the result $p_c = 0.5$ is. Suppose, $p = 0.45 < p_c$. This means that if N is large, then we will almost never see an uncontained spread of wildfire. It will spontaneously stop after running out of paths forward. Or, if we would rather think of an epidemic spread, the infection will spontaneously run out of carriers. But... every vertex of the grid has four edges emanating from it. If a vertex represents a person, then the open edges correspond to paths for the infection to spread to other people. And if $p = 0.45$, which is close to a half, then on average each vertex in the grid has around two open paths. So each infected person should be able to infect, again on average, two uninfected neighbors. Should it not mean that the infection will grow "exponentially", and fill the grid?

Well, a theorem is a fact, so this intuition must be wrong. To get an insight of what actually happens, look at the two simulations in Figure 37, both on the grid with $N = 50$. The first one is for $p = 0.45$, and the second one is for $p = 0.55$. The first grid splits into *clusters* connected by open edges in the grid. Each cluster is isolated from its neighboring clusters, as there is no open path connecting them. The clusters are indicated by different colors. Notice that all of them are relatively small compared to the overall size of the grid, and none of them spans the whole height of the grid. Such clustering is a well-known feature of social networks, and it makes an intuitive sense. Yes, each person in a cluster, on average, has around two "close contacts" – but all of them come from the same group of "friends". It is remarkable, that a simple model captures it. It is also remarkable as to what it suggests about the spread of wildfire or disease: if a critical probability is not reached, then the spread will consume a cluster, and then die out of its own.

The second picture, in contrast, is dominated by one huge cluster which takes up almost all of the grid – if the critical probability is exceeded, then wildfire will consume everything.

Figure 37. Simulating percolation on a 50×50 grid. Top: $p = 0.45$, bottom: $p = 0.55$. Connected clusters marked with different colors.

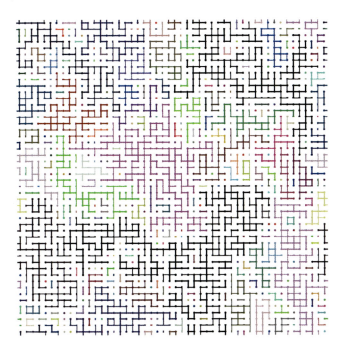

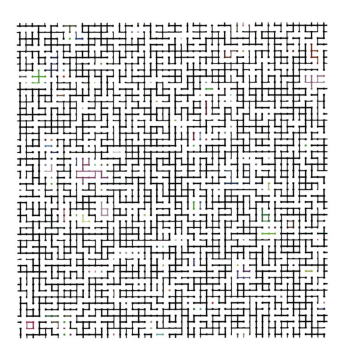

6.3. It's a small world after all

There is an obvious difference between the spread of a wildfire in a forest
and that of a respiratory infection in a city. A tree cannot get on a bus, or
go to a concert, or to school. A fire can only spread between neighboring
trees. Sporadic "long-distance" interactions are a distinguishing feature
of human social networks, and can play a key role in epidemic spread,
depending on the nature of the infection. There are various ways to modify
a "nearest neighbor" interaction model to add this feature. For instance,
consider again our percolation model with an $N \times N$ square grid. There are
$(N + 1)^2/2$ *pairs* of nodes in the grid. Let us select some small probability
$q > 0$, randomly pick a q-th fraction of the pairs (that is, $q(N + 1)^2/2$ in
total) – and connect them with shortcut links. This will have the effect
of connecting some of the percolation clusters, and will lower the critical
probability. In fact, it can be shown [Ne02] that in this model, for small
values of q,

$$p_c \approx \frac{1}{2} - q^{\frac{18}{43}}.$$

This is a substantial change: for $q = 0.01$ it would lower the threshold probability p_c from 0.5 to about 0.35, so controlling "long-distance" interactions
becomes key for a practical control of an epidemic with such a mode of
spread.

Networks which feature long-distance connection in addition to near
neighbor interactions are known in the literature as *small world networks*
[WaSt98]. If you would like a little light reading on this, I would recommend a survey [KeEa05] for a discussion of network models in epidemic
spread. One important feature of small world networks is an emergence
of "super-spreaders": nodes from which an infection can spread to many
clusters.

To discuss it, let us introduce the following terminology: the *degree* of
a node in a social network is the number of edges (connections) from this
node to other nodes in the network. In real-life social networks, the value of
the degree is distributed very unevenly. If we denote $P(d)$ the proportion of
the nodes in the network, whose degree is d, then it often follows a power
law:

$$P(d) \approx \text{const} \cdot d^{-\tau},$$

where the power τ usually is (for mysterious reasons) a number between 2 and 3 [**Dor00**]. Networks with such a power law abound in the literature, including such disparate examples as collaboration networks of authors of academic papers, and the World Wide Web. Think of this as an extreme manifestation of Pareto's Principle: *a small proportion of the nodes is responsible for a vast proportion of the connections*. In an epidemic which spreads through a network of social interactions, these nodes are the super-spreaders, and will similarly be responsible for most of the infections. Speaking informally, once most of these super-spreader nodes become infected, and become either isolated or immune, and can no longer spread the infection, the epidemic will rapidly subside.

> *Pareto's Principle* sometimes also known as *80/20 rule* is named after an economist V. Pareto, who calculated that, in the end of the 1800's, about 80% of all land in Italy was owned by 20% of the population, and then, to his surprise, discovered that a similar ratio held in several other countries. The general principle can be formulated as "80% of the effects are due to 20% of the causes" and is quite ubiquitous (although the specific ratio 80/20 can, of course, change). It applies, for example, to the distribution of wealth, the proportion of patients consuming most of the hospital resources, and, as mentioned above, human social networks. Pareto's Principle reflects a growth scenario, known as *preferential attachment*. To see the idea, consider how the investments would grow for a group of investors. Of course, there will be random fluctuations in the growth, but on average, the annual growth will be proportional to the current size of the investment. Thus, the growth would not be uniform – most growth would attach to the largest investments (hence, the name "preferential attachment"). Such a scenario leads to a statistical distribution quantifying Pareto's Principle. It is very plausible that preferential attachment drives the growth of human social networks – i.e. the more social connections we already have, the more new ones we are likely to develop over a period of time.

In practical modeling applications, the SIR model and other compartmentalized models provide a good *qualitative* understanding of the dynamic of an epidemic, with the now canonical picture of a wave of infections, which crests and then recedes as the pool of susceptible members of the population is depleted. However, when it comes to *quantitative* predictions (such as when does the wave peak, what proportion of the population will get infected, etc), the assumption of uniform mixing of the population, in which infected members are indistinguishable is too simplistic, and can lead to radically inflated numbers.

Notably, it was a poor match to the data after the outbreak of SARS in 2003, for instance: it was suggested in the literature that super-spreaders played a key role in that epidemic, and small-world models such as **[Sm06]** were proposed to account for this effect. More recently, a similar explanation was offered to explain the data from Covid-19 epidemic, and, in particular, why the proportion of the population infected in an epidemic wave would be substantially smaller than suggested by a compartmentalized model. Of note is a paper **[Gom20]** which combines a compartmentalized model approach with a version of Pareto's Principle of infectiousness of individuals to fit the data (a somewhat simplified expose of this is **[Lew20]**).

6.3.1. Making quantitative predictions: the ubiquitous Mr. Gompertz. The models of epidemic spread we have considered so far are extremely helpful in building our intuition about the spread of an infectious disease, but they are notoriously unreliable when it comes to *real-time* numerical predictions about the course of an epidemic. This was thrown into the spotlight recently, in the early days of COVID-19 pandemic, when the predictions of the models often diverged with reality. This is hardly a new phenomenon, and a previous notable instance is the modeling of the spread of SARS, which I have already mentioned above. Why is this the case? Firstly, the models themselves are rather complex, and in particular, non-linear. Their predictions can change quite drastically under very small changes of the parameters. The quality of the data itself is another problem, as these types of models tend to be quite sensitive to "noise" (this, of course, can be a problem for most predictive models, known by practitioners as "garbage in, garbage out").

Instead of trying to construct a "realistic" dynamical model of epidemic spread, we could attempt to find a nicely fitting *empirical* formula. Such empirical modeling is a way of letting the numbers speak for themselves, rather than trying to force them to fit our likely flawed theoretical understanding. A notable example is the recent use of our old friend, the the Gompertz function from §3.3 to match the data for the COVID-19 pandemic. This, to my knowledge, was first suggested by M. Levitt **[Lev20]**.

To see an example of such a fit, look at the graphs in Figure 38 which I made using the data freely available from *ourworldindata.org*. They concern the death statistics for the Spring 2020 wave of COVID-19 pandemic from Sweden (above) and the UK (below). Death statistics is more reliable than case statistics (the latter can change quite drastically with the testing policy and availability of tests). The two countries were chosen because both of them have reliable and timely death reporting systems. In the figure, $D(t)$ is the cumulative number of deaths occuring on day t. The scatterplots show

$$\ln\left(\frac{d\ln D(t)}{dt}\right) = \ln\left(\frac{D'(t)}{D(t)}\right).$$

Of course, deaths are recorded daily, so instead of the continuous quantity $D'(t)$ I used the discrete one $\Delta D(t)$ which recorded new deaths per day. [1] Note that each scatterplot nicely aligns along a straight line, suggesting the relation

(6.3.1) $$\log\frac{d}{dt}\log D(t) = q - mt \text{ (compare this with 6.3.1).}$$

The solution of this Gompertz equation is

(6.3.2) $$D(t) = D_0 \exp\left(\frac{\exp(q)}{m}(1 - \exp(-mt))\right),$$

giving a simple formula for a good quantitative prediction.

There is an obvious practical advantage in trying to fit a Gompertz law (6.3.1) to the data, rather than the output of an SIR model, since we only need to know the slope and the y-intercept of the straight line with the best fit (calculated, for instance, using the least square method, which is standard in Stats). I was able to do my calculations with freely available data, and an Excel spreadsheet in literally ten minutes – and given data of a reasonable quality, these predictions seem robust (the straight lines would not change much if you try to fit them to different parts of the scatterplots).

Why Gompertz? Imagine, that at the initial stage of an outbreak the infection is so rare that each infected individual would only come in contact with susceptible ones. Think of starting a percolation model with infected dots scattered in the grid far from each other. If we assume for simplicity that each infected person comes in contact daily with roughly the same number of "neighbors" (think of a percolation model again) and has a non-zero chance of infecting each of them then the initial daily growth of the *cumulative* number $C(t)$ of infected people will be given by

$$\Delta C = kC,$$

where

$k = $ (average number of contacts) $\times$ (probability of transmission) > 0.

Replacing ΔC with C', we get $C' = kC$: this is the recipe for an exponential growth, which is what the initial spread of an infection through the population looks like. However, this model implies that a fixed percentage of "neighbors" of every infected individual become infected (and thus are no longer susceptible) each day. The correct formula for k should read:

$k = $ (average number of susceptible contacts) $\times$ (probability of transmission),

---

[1] One justification for considering the ratio of daily deaths to cumulative deaths at the end of the day (or daily cases divided by the cumulative cases at the end of the day, if reliable case data were available) is that if the epidemic growth was governed by the exponential law $\exp(rt)$ then such a ratio would be close to r. So we can say that we are trying to measure changes in the exponential rate of the spread.

Figure 38. Fitting $\ln(d\ln(D(t))/D(t))$ to a straight line, where $D(t)$ is the number of deaths from COVID-19 recorded on day t from the first recorded death. Top: Sweden, bottom: the UK.

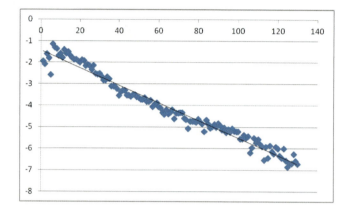

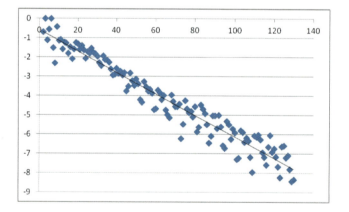

and while the second multiple is fixed, the first one decreases daily – by the *same proportion*. This means that $k = k(t)$ is an exponentially decreasing function, or, in other words,

$$\ln(k(t)) = \ln\left(\frac{C'(t)}{C(t)}\right)$$

is a linearly decreasing function, which is, of course, the Gompertz law.

In view of this, when plotting the graph of $C(t)$ (or $D(t)$ when the reliable data on $C(t)$ is not available) we should expect a graph which starts as an exponential function, and then levels off exponentially fast as the susceptible population is depleted and the outbreak dies down due to lack of people to

Figure 39. Gompertz-type dynamics in a SIR model. (a) $C(t) = 1000 - S(t)$, the cumulative total of infected; (b) $I(t)$; (c) $\ln(C'(t)/C(t))$.

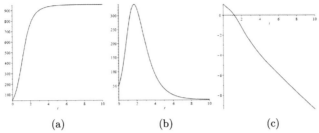

(a)   (b)   (c)

infect. This is how a Gompertz growth behaves (see the discussion at the end of §3.3).

In fact, the good old SIR model exhibits a very Gompertz-like behaviour. Have a look at Figure 39 in which we consider a very simple SIR model with the following parameters. We set $\delta = 0$ (the epidemic is too short to be affected by the natural growth and death rate of the population), $\gamma = 1$, and $\beta = 3.2$ (for $R_0 = 3.2$). The population size is $N = 1000$, and since $\delta = 0$, eventually the infection will disappear from the population in the SIR model.

We seed the population with 50 infected members ($I(0) = 50$, $S(0) = 950$). Note that at any given time t, the cumulative number of exposed members is

$$C(t) = 1000 - S(t).$$

As you can see in Figure 39, the decrease of $\ln(C'(t)/C(t))$ is very nearly linear, so in practice, it is difficult to tell the difference from the Gompertz model.

**Exercises for
Chapter 6**

1. **An SIR model with treatment.** Suppose that, on average, a proportion $\eta \in (0,1)$ of the infected population gets treatment, which does not affect the infectiousness, but does reduce the mean recovery time from $1/\gamma_u$ for the untreated individuals to $1/\gamma_t < 1/\gamma_u$ for the treated ones.

   Assume, for simplicity, that the birth rate and the death rate are both equal to zero (this is not a realistic assumption, of course, but it is an acceptable simplicfication if both are low) and formulate an SIR model which describes this situation. How does the value of R_0 change in this model, compared to the case when no treatment is available?

2. **Vertical transmission of disease.** Some infections (such as rubella, herpes, or HIV) can be passed from a mother to a child. This is known as *vertical transmission*. Formulate an SIR model for such an infection. For simplicity, assume that half of the population, and, in particular, half of the newborns are female, and make the model describe the female population only.

3. Verify the calculations (6.1.8) and (6.1.9).

4. **Imitating a small world network connectivity in an SIR model.** Consider the following very simplistic scenario: 90% of the population has 10 times fewer social connections than the remaining 10%. The recovery rate is $\gamma = 0.3$, the birth/death rate is $\delta = 0$ (not a realistic assumption, of course, we are just ignoring the natural changes in the population size for the period of the epidemic), the size of the population is $N = 1000$. Finally, the rate at which the "superpreaders" in the population are contagious is a scary $\beta = 10$.

   (a) Write the equations of the compartmental SIR model with two subpopulations.

(b) Use a computer algebra system to simulate the course of the epidemic starting with 100 infections. Determine the size of the population which avoids being infected.

References for Chapter 6

[Dor00]   Dorogovtsev S.N., Mendes J.F., Samukhin A.N., *Structure of growing networks with preferential linking.* Phys Rev Lett. **85**(2000), 4633-6.

[Gom20]   G.M. Gomes, R.M. Corder, J.G. King, K.E. Langwig, C. Souto-Maior, J. Carneiro, G. Goncalves, C. Penha-Goncalves, M.U. Ferreira, R. Aguas *Individual variation in susceptibility or exposure to SARS-CoV-2 lowers the herd immunity threshold,* e-print medRxiv, 2020

[KeEa05]   M.J. Keeling, K.T.D. Eames, *Networks and epidemic models,* J. R. Soc. Interface **2**(2005), 295–307

[KeMcK27]   W.O. Kermack, A.G. McKendrick, *A Contribution to the Mathematical Theory of Epidemics,* Proceedings of the Royal Society A. **115**(1927) 700–721.

[Lev20]   M. Levitt, A. Scaiewicz, F. Zonta, *Predicting the Trajectory of Any COVID-19 Epidemic From the Best Straight Line,* e-print medRxiv, 2020

[Lour20]   Lourenco, J., Paton, R., Ghafari, M., Kraemer, M., Thompson, C., Simmonds, P., Klenerman, P., Gupta, S., *Fundamental principles of epidemic spread highlight the immediate need for large-scale serological surveys to assess the stage of the SARS-CoV-2 epidemic,* e-print medRxiv, 2020

[Ne02]   M.E.J. Newman, I. Jensen, R.M. Ziff, *Percolation and epidemics in a two-dimensional small world,* Phys. Rev. E, **65**(2002), 021904

[Lew20]   N. Lewis, *Why herd immunity to COVID-19 is reached much earlier than thought,* available from *nicholaslewis.org*

[Rid14]   Ridenhour, B., Kowalik, J. M., Shay, D. K. *Unraveling R_0: considerations for public health applications.* American journal of public health, **104**(2014), e32–41.

[Sm06]   M. Small, C.K. Tse, D.M. Walker, *Super-spreaders and the rate of transmission of the SARS virus,* Physica D: Nonlinear Phenomena, **215**(2006), 146-158

[WaSt98]   D. J. Watts, S. H. Strogatz, *Collective dynamics of "small-world" networks.* Nature **393**(1998), 440–442

Chapter 7

Solutions of selected problems

Chapter 1

Problem 1. We have

$$x_{n+1} = (n+1)x_n, \text{ and } x_0 = 1.$$

The next few terms are $x_1 = 1 \cdot x_0 = 1$, $x_2 = 2 \cdot x_1 = 2$, $x_3 = 3 \cdot x_2 = 6$, and so on. We recognize that

(7.0.1) $$x_n = n!$$

We can easily prove this formula by induction. If we assume that $x_n = n!$ then $x_{n+1} = (n+1)x_n = (n+1)n! = (n+1)!$ as required.

Problem 2. (a)

$$x_{n+2} = 4x_{n+1} - 3x_n.$$

The characteristic equation is

$$\lambda^2 = 4\lambda - 3, \text{ or } \lambda^2 - 4\lambda + 3 = 0.$$

The roots are $\lambda_1 = 1$, $\lambda_2 = 3$. The general solution is

$$x_n = c_1 + 3^n c_2.$$

(b)

$$x_{n+1} = -4x_n - 8x_{n-1}.$$

The characteristic equation is

$$\lambda^2 = -4\lambda - 8,$$

$$(\lambda + 2)^2 = -4,$$

the roots are $\lambda_1 = -2 + 2i$, $\lambda_2 = -2 - 2i$. We have

$$\lambda_1 = 2\sqrt{2}\left(\cos\frac{3\pi}{4} + i\sin\frac{3\pi}{4}\right),$$

so

$$x_n = c_1(2\sqrt{2})^n \cos\frac{3\pi n}{4} + c_2(2\sqrt{2})^n \sin\frac{3\pi n}{4}.$$

(c)

$$x_{n+2} = 3x_{n+1} - 3x_n + x_{n-1}.$$

The characteristic equation is

$$\lambda^3 = 3\lambda^2 - 3\lambda + 1,$$

$$(\lambda - 1)^3 = 0.$$

There is a single root $\lambda = 1$ of multiplicity 3. The general solution is

$$x_n = c_1 + nc_2 + n^2 c_3.$$

Problem 3. (a) From the previous solution,

$$x_n = c_1 + 3^n c_2.$$

Substituting the initial data, we get

$$\begin{cases} c_1 + c_2 = 1 \\ c_1 + 3c_2 = 2 \end{cases}$$

Solving it, we get $c_1 = 0.5$, $c_2 = 0.5$, so

$$x_n = 0.5(1 + 3^n).$$

(b) The general solution is

$$x_n = c_1(2\sqrt{2})^n \cos\frac{3\pi n}{4} + c_2(2\sqrt{2})^n \sin\frac{3\pi n}{4}.$$

From the initial data, we get the system

$$\begin{cases} c_1 = 1 \\ -2c_1 + 2c_2 = 1 \end{cases}$$

Thus, $c_2 = \frac{3}{2}$, and

$$x_n = (2\sqrt{2})^n \cos\frac{3\pi n}{4} + \left(\frac{3}{2}\right)(2\sqrt{2})^n \sin\frac{3\pi n}{4}.$$

(c) From

$$x_n = c_1 + nc_2 + n^2 c_3$$

we get

$$\begin{cases} c_1 = 1 \\ c_1 + c_2 + c_3 = 1 \\ c_1 + 2c_2 + 4c_3 = -1 \end{cases}$$

We have $c_1 = 1$, $c_2 = 1$, $c_3 = -1$, and

$$x_n = 1 + n - n^2.$$

Problem 4. The equation is

$$x_{n+1} = x_n + x_{n-1} - 2, \ n \geq 2, \ x_1 = 1, \ x_2 = 2.$$

We have $x_3 = 1$, $x_4 = 1$, and $x_5 = 0$. This means that the harvesting leads to the extinction of the population after 5 months, so $x_{12} = 0$.

Problem 5. (a) The characteristic equation is

$$\lambda^3 = \lambda^2 + \lambda - 1.$$

We can guess one root $\lambda = 1$ and factor out $\lambda - 1$:

$$\lambda^3 - \lambda^2 - \lambda + 1 = (\lambda - 1)(\lambda^2 - 1) = (\lambda - 1)^2(\lambda + 1).$$

The general solution is

$$x_n = c_1 + nc_2 + (-1)^n c_3.$$

(b) We have

$$\begin{cases} c_1 + c_3 = 1 \\ c_1 + c_2 - c_3 = 1 \\ c_1 + 2c_2 + c_3 = 2 \end{cases}$$

Hence, $c_1 = 0.75$, $c_2 = 0.5$, $c_3 = 0.25$, and

$$x_n = 0.75 + 0.5n + 0.25(-1)^n.$$

Problem 6. Your *last* step will cover either one or two stairs. In the first case, you will go from $n - 1$-st stair to the n-th one. There are S_{n-1} ways to get to the $n - 1$-st stair, so there are S_{n-1} ways to climb n stairs *if you take one stair with your last step*. In the second case, you will go from $n - 2$-nd stair to the n-th one. There are S_{n-2} ways to get to the $n - 2$-nd stair, so there are S_{n-2} ways to climb n stairs *if you take two stairs with your last step*. Altogether, we get

$$S_n = S_{n-1} + S_{n-2}.$$

Problem 7.

(a) The characteristic equation is

$$\lambda^3 = \lambda^2 + \lambda + 1.$$

(b) Since the roots are distinct, the the general solution will have the form
$x_n = c_1\phi^n + c_2\psi^n + c_3\theta^n$.

(c) We get the following system of equations for c_1, c_2, c_3:

$$\begin{cases} c_1 + c_2 + c_3 = 0 \\ c_1\phi + c_2\psi + c_3\theta = 0 \\ c_1\phi^2 + c_2\psi^2 + c_3\theta^2 = 1 \end{cases}$$

We are in for a Linear Algebra treat. Let us start by using the first equation to get rid of c_1 in the other two:

$$\begin{cases} c_2(\psi - \phi) + c_3(\theta - \phi) = 0 \\ c_2(\psi^2 - \phi^2) + c_3(\theta^2 - \phi^2) = 1 \end{cases}$$

Note that $\psi^2 - \phi^2 = (\psi - \phi)(\psi + \phi)$, so if we mutiply the first line by $(\psi + \phi)$, we get

$$c_2(\psi^2 - \phi^2) + c_3(\theta - \phi)(\psi + \phi) = 0.$$

Subtracting this from the second line, we get a formula for c_3:

$$c_3\left[(\theta^2 - \phi^2) - (\theta - \phi)(\psi + \phi)\right] = 1, \text{ or}$$

$$c_3 = \frac{1}{(\theta - \phi)(\theta - \psi)}.$$

By symmetry of the problem (explain!) this gives

$$c_1 = \frac{1}{(\phi - \psi)(\phi - \theta)} \text{ and } c_2 = \frac{1}{(\psi - \phi)(\psi - \theta)}.$$

The (rather nice looking) formula for x_n is:

$$x_n = \frac{1}{(\phi - \psi)(\phi - \theta)}\phi^n + \frac{1}{(\psi - \phi)(\psi - \theta)}\psi^n + \frac{1}{(\theta - \phi)(\theta - \psi)}\theta^n.$$

(d) Using a computer algebra system we find that the characteristic equation has three distinct roots, approximately equal to

$$1.83928, \quad -0.41964 + 0.60629i, \quad -0.41964 - 0.60629i.$$

Let us set

$$\phi \approx 1.83928, \quad \psi \approx -0.41964 + 0.60629i, \quad \text{and } \theta \approx -0.41964 - 0.60629i.$$

Plugging this into the above formula for x_n and rounding off to an integer, we get

$$x_{12} = 274.$$

(e) The root with the largest modulus is $\phi \approx 1.83928$. Since $c_1 \neq 0$, the power ϕ^n will take over and $x_n \sim \phi^n$. Thus,

$$\lim_{n \to \infty} \frac{x_{n+1}}{x_n} = \phi \approx 1.83928.$$

Problem 8. We use the formula (1.4.3):

$$P_n = a^n P_0 - \frac{a^n - 1}{a - 1}r.$$

In the case (a) it gives

$$P_n = \left(\frac{1}{4}\right)^n - \frac{\left(\frac{1}{4}\right)^n - 1}{\frac{1}{4} - 1} = \frac{7}{3}\left(\frac{1}{4}\right)^n - \frac{4}{3}.$$

Similarly in the case (b) we get

$$P_n = 2^n \frac{1}{2} - \frac{1}{4}\frac{2^n - 1}{2 - 1} = \frac{1}{4}2^n + \frac{1}{4} = 2^{n-2} + \frac{1}{4}.$$

Problem 9. The formula (1.4.3) cannot be applied since in this case $a = 1$ so the geometric series formula cannot be used. But the calculation is quite trivial:

$x_1 = x_0 - r$

$x_2 = x_1 - r = x_0 - 2r$

$x_3 = x_2 - r = x_0 - 3r$

. . .

$x_n = x_0 - nr.$

Problem 10. The equation $x_n = x_{n-2} + 4$ is non-homogenous. To solve it we will first find the general solution of the corresponding homogenous equation $x_n = x_{n-2}$ and then will try to 'guess' a particular solution of the non-homogenous equation $x_n = x_{n-2} + 4$.

Let us start with $x_n = x_{n-2}$; it can be solved by following the standard algorithm. $\lambda^2 = 1$ is the characteristic equation with two real solutions $1, -1$. So

$$x_n^h = c_1 1^n + c_2(-1)^n = c_1 + c_2(-1)^n.$$

Notice, that this formula is a fancy way of saying that all even-numbered values of the sequence are equal (to $c_1 + c_2$), and all odd-numbered values are equal as well (to $c_1 - c_2$).

It is a tough problem to find a particular solution to a non-homogenous equation. Here is a useful trick to solve it in our case. We note that to ensure that the value of x_n is incremented by 4 after two steps of the sequence, it is enough to ensure that it is incremented by 2 after one step of the sequence. In other words, our non-homogeneous equation follows from the system

$$\begin{cases} x_n = x_{n-1} + 2 \\ x_{n-1} = x_{n-2} + 2 \end{cases}$$

(of course, the system does not follow from the equation).

The system contains two copies of the same equation, just with different indexing. The equation $x_n = x_{n-1} + 2$ has the solution

$$x_n^{nh} = x_0 + 2n$$

which solves the original equation. Indeed, if we substitute $x_n = x_0 + 2n$ and $x_{n-2} = x_0 + 2(n-2)$ into $x_n = x_{n-2} + 4$ we get the correct equality

$$x_0 + 2n = x_0 + 2n - 4 + 4.$$

Finally the general solution is

$$x_n = x_n^h + x_n^{nh} = c_1 + c_2(-1)^n + x_0 + 2n$$

(there are three parameters here instead of two, which means that their values are related). Now we can apply the initial conditions $x_0 = 1$, $x_1 = 3$:

$$\begin{cases} 1 = x_0 = c_1 + c_2 + 1 + 0 \\ 3 = x_1 = c_1 - c_2 + 1 + 2 \end{cases}$$

So $c_1 = 0, c_2 = 0$ and $x_n = 1 + 2n$.

Problem 11. To calculate e^A we apply matrix power series formula

$$e^A = \sum_{n=0}^{\infty} \frac{1}{n!} A^n = I + A + \frac{1}{2}A^2 + \frac{1}{6}A^3 + \dots$$

$$A^2 = \begin{pmatrix} 0 & 0 & 1 \\ 0 & 0 & 0 \\ 0 & 0 & 0 \end{pmatrix}.$$

$$A^3 = \begin{pmatrix} 0 & 0 & 0 \\ 0 & 0 & 0 \\ 0 & 0 & 0 \end{pmatrix},$$

i.e. A^3 is the zero matrix as well as all higher degrees $A^n = 0, n > 2$. So

$$e^A = \begin{pmatrix} 1 & 0 & 0 \\ 0 & 1 & 0 \\ 0 & 0 & 1 \end{pmatrix} + \begin{pmatrix} 0 & 1 & 0 \\ 0 & 0 & 1 \\ 0 & 0 & 0 \end{pmatrix} + \frac{1}{2}\begin{pmatrix} 0 & 0 & 1 \\ 0 & 0 & 0 \\ 0 & 0 & 0 \end{pmatrix} = \begin{pmatrix} 1 & 1 & \frac{1}{2} \\ 0 & 1 & 1 \\ 0 & 0 & 1 \end{pmatrix}$$

Problem 12.

(a) 1, 1, 2, 2.

(b) Let us denote v_n the number of newborn rabbits in month n, w_n the number of 1-month olds, and z_n the number of 2-month olds. Then

$$x_n = v_n + w_n + z_n.$$

We have the following equations:

$$\begin{cases} v_{n+1} = w_n + z_n \\ w_{n+1} = v_n \\ z_{n+1} = w_n \end{cases}$$

Applying them repeatedly, we easily get

$$x_{n+2} = 2v_n + 2w_n + z_n,$$

$$x_{n+3} = 2v_n + 3w_n + 2z_n, \text{ and}$$

$$x_{n+4} = 3v_n + 4w_n + 2z_n = x_{n+3} + x_{n+2} - x_n.$$

Chapter 2

Problem 1. The life cycle graph is seen in Figure 40. The matrix is

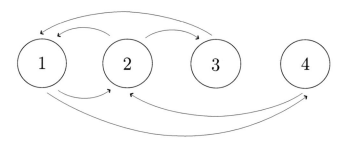

Figure 40. The life cycle graph for Problem 1

irreducible. Consider, for example, the following looped path in the life cycle graph:

$$1 \mapsto 4 \mapsto 2 \mapsto 3 \mapsto 1.$$

You can use it to visit any node starting from any other node.

Problem 2.

(a) The matrix A has eigenvalues $\lambda_1 = -5$, $\lambda_2 = 2$ with eigenvectors

$$V_1 = \begin{pmatrix} -1 \\ 3 \end{pmatrix}, V_2 = \begin{pmatrix} 2 \\ 1 \end{pmatrix}.$$

So

$$X_n = c_1(-5)^n V_1 + c_2 2^n V_2 = \begin{pmatrix} -c_1(-5)^n + 2c_2 2^n \\ 3c_1(-5)^n + c_2 2^n \end{pmatrix}.$$

(b) The matrix is upper-triangular, so its eigenvalues are the terms on the diagonal: $\lambda_1 = -1$, $\lambda_2 = 3$, $\lambda_3 = 1$ (verify by writing the characteristic equation). For $\lambda_1 = -1$ we get the following system of equations to find an eigenvector V_1:

$$\begin{bmatrix} 0 & 1 & 2 \\ 0 & 4 & 1 \\ 0 & 0 & 2 \end{bmatrix} \begin{bmatrix} v_1 \\ v_2 \\ v_3 \end{bmatrix} = 0.$$

This is satisfied by any vector with $v_2 = v_3 = 0$, so we set

$$V_1 = \begin{bmatrix} 1 \\ 0 \\ 0 \end{bmatrix}.$$

Similarly, we find

$$V_2 = \begin{bmatrix} 1 \\ 4 \\ 0 \end{bmatrix}, \text{ and } V_3 = \begin{bmatrix} -1.5 \\ 1 \\ -2 \end{bmatrix}.$$

The end result is

$$X_n = c_1(-1)^n V_1 + c_2 3^n V_2 + c_3 1^n V_3, \text{ or}$$

$$\begin{bmatrix} x_1 \\ x_2 \\ x_3 \end{bmatrix} = \begin{bmatrix} (-1)^n c_1 + 3^n c_2 - 1.5 c_3 \\ 4 \cdot 3^n c_2 + c_3 \\ -2 c_3 \end{bmatrix}.$$

Problem 3. Let us find the spectral radius of the matrix A. The characteristic equation is

$$|A - \lambda I| = 0$$

$$\begin{vmatrix} \frac{1}{2} - \lambda & \frac{1}{4} & 0 \\ \frac{1}{4} & \frac{1}{2} - \lambda & \frac{1}{4} \\ 0 & \frac{1}{4} & \frac{1}{2} - \lambda \end{vmatrix} = 0,$$

$$\left(\frac{1}{2} - \lambda\right)^3 - \frac{1}{8}\left(\frac{1}{2} - \lambda\right) = 0.$$

Factoring out $\frac{1}{2} - \lambda$, we obtain

$$\left(\frac{1}{2} - \lambda\right)\left(\lambda^2 - \lambda + \frac{1}{8}\right) = 0.$$

The roots of the equation are

$$\frac{1}{2}, \frac{2 + \sqrt{2}}{4}, \frac{2 - \sqrt{2}}{4}.$$

The second eigenvalue has the largest modulus, so

$$\rho(A) = \frac{2 + \sqrt{2}}{4}.$$

Since $\sqrt{2} < 2$, $\rho(A) < 1$ (using a calculator we can get the approximate value $\rho(A) \approx 0.853$. Hence

$$A^n \xrightarrow[n \to \infty]{} 0.$$

Problem 4.

(a) Let us denote $x_{1,n}$ the number of fry in the n-th year. $x_{2,n}$ will stand for smolts, and $x_{3,n}$ for adults. Each year, 20% of the adults will be spawning females, each laying 2000 eggs, which will become 200 fry. This gives us the equation

$$x_{1,n} = 0.2x_{3,n-1} \times 200 = 40x_{3,n-1}.$$

Only 10% of fry become new smolts, contributing $0.1x_{1,n-1}$ to $x_{2,n}$. What proportion of smolts is new, as opposed to one year old? The annual survival rate at this stage is 0.7. This means that there will be 0.7 one year old smolts for each new one, and hence, the proportion of one year old smolts is $0.7/(1+0.7) \approx 0.41$, so the proportion of new smolts is around 0.59 of all smolts.

We thus get the equation

$$x_{2,n} = 0.1x_{1,n-1} + 0.7 \times 0.59x_{2,n-1}.$$

Finally,

$$x_{3,n} = 0.7 \times 0.41x_{2,n-1} + 0.6 \times 0.8x_{3,n-1}.$$

So

$$X_n = AX_{n-1}$$

with

$$A = \begin{pmatrix} 0 & 0 & 40 \\ 0.1 & 0.413 & 0 \\ 0 & 0.287 & 0.48 \end{pmatrix}$$

(b) Using a computer algebra system, we find that A has eigenvalues approximately equal to

$$-0.235 + 0.886i, \quad -0.235 - 0.886i, \quad 1.364.$$

The dominant eigenvalue is $\lambda \approx 1.364 > 1$ (we do not actually need to compare moduli of the eigenvalues to know this: since it is the only positive eigenvalue, it must be the dominant one by Perron-Frobenius Theorem). Hence, the population is going to grow with time.

(c) The normalized eigenvector which corresponds to λ has approximate coordinates

$$[0.878, 0.092, 0.030].$$

With time, the ratio of the number of fry to adults will converge to

$$\frac{0.878}{0.03} \approx 29.27.$$

Problem 5. Let us first fix the indexes:

$$y_{n+1} = 67y_{n-3} + 4y_{n-2} + 55y_n.$$

We now define new variables as $x_{1,n} = y_{n-3}, x_{2,n} = y_{n-2}, x_{3,n} = y_{n-1}, x_{4,n} = y_n$, so the original equation may be rewritten as the system

$$\begin{cases} x_{1,n+1} = x_{2,n} \\ x_{2,n+1} = x_{3,n} \\ x_{3,n+1} = x_{4,n} \\ x_{4,n+1} = 67x_{1,n} + 4x_{2,n} + 55x_{4,n} \end{cases}$$

or, in the matrix form,

$$\begin{pmatrix} x_{1,n+1} \\ x_{2,n+1} \\ x_{3,n+1} \\ x_{4,n+1} \end{pmatrix} = \begin{pmatrix} 0 & 1 & 0 & 0 \\ 0 & 0 & 1 & 0 \\ 0 & 0 & 0 & 1 \\ 67 & 4 & 0 & 55 \end{pmatrix} \begin{pmatrix} x_{1,n} \\ x_{2,n} \\ x_{3,n} \\ x_{4,n} \end{pmatrix}$$

Problem 6.

(a) Let us write down a system of difference equations, in which $x_{j,n}$ corresponds the number of surfers visiting the j-th page at the n-th moment of time.

$$\begin{cases} x_{1,n+1} = x_{4,n} \\ x_{2,n+1} = \frac{1}{2}x_{1,n} + \frac{1}{2}x_{3,n} + \frac{1}{3}x_{5,n} \\ x_{3,n+1} = \frac{1}{3}x_{2,n} + x_{6,n} \\ x_{4,n+1} = \frac{1}{3}x_{5,n} \\ x_{5,n+1} = \frac{1}{2}x_{1,n} + \frac{1}{3}x_{2,n} \\ x_{6,n+1} = \frac{1}{3}x_{2,n} + \frac{1}{2}x_{3,n} + \frac{1}{3}x_{5,n} \end{cases}$$

or $X_{n+1} = AX_n$, where

$$A = \begin{pmatrix} 0 & 0 & 0 & 1 & 0 & 0 \\ \frac{1}{2} & 0 & \frac{1}{2} & 0 & \frac{1}{3} & 0 \\ 0 & \frac{1}{3} & 0 & 0 & 0 & 1 \\ 0 & 0 & 0 & 0 & \frac{1}{3} & 0 \\ \frac{1}{2} & \frac{1}{3} & 0 & 0 & 0 & 0 \\ 0 & \frac{1}{3} & \frac{1}{2} & 0 & \frac{1}{3} & 0 \end{pmatrix}$$

(b) The graph of the network is strongly connected, since there is a path from any page to any other page. Hence, A is an irreducible matrix. Since it has non-negative terms, Perron-Frobenius Theorem applies.

(c) The eigenvalue of A with the largest modulus is 1 and the corresponding eigenvector is

$$[1, 15/2, 12, 1, 3, 19/2].$$

The order of the six web pages in order of decreasing importance is: 3,
6, 2, 5, 1, and 4 (the last two have an equal rank).

Problem 7. Figure 7 shows the life cycle graph of the seeds; the number next to each arrow indicates the corresponding proportion (or the multiple). Indeed, let us denote $s_{1,n}$, $s_{2,n}$, $s_{3,n}$ the number of new seeds, 1-year
old seeds, and 2-year old seeds correspondingly in year n. Then $\sigma s_{1,n}$ will
survive to contribute to $s_{2,n+1}$. Of $s_{2,n}$, the proportion of α will germinate
and produce γ seeds each, contributing $\alpha\gamma s_{2,n}$ to $s_{1,n+1}$. Of the remaining
$(1 - \alpha)s_{2,n}$ 1-year old seeds, $\sigma(1 - \alpha)s_{2,n}$ will survive the winter and contribute to $s_{3,n+1}$. And finally, $\beta\gamma s_{3,n}$ new seeds will be produced by the
2-year old seeds.

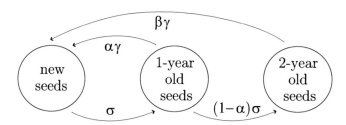

Figure 41. The life cycle graph of the seeds in Problem 7

This diagram translates into the following Leslie matrix:

$$\begin{bmatrix} 0 & \alpha\gamma & \beta\gamma \\ \sigma & 0 & 0 \\ 0 & (1 - \alpha)\sigma & 0 \end{bmatrix}$$

Problem 8.

(a) The possible parental genotype combinations are (AA, AA), (Aa, Aa),
and (AA, Aa):
  - (AA, AA) produces type AA with frequency u_n^2;
  - (Aa, Aa) produces AA with frequency $0.25v_n^2$ and Aa with fre-
    quency $0.5v_n^2$ (the combinations aa are possible but not viable);

– (AA, Aa) produces AA with frequency $u_n v_n$ and Aa also with frequency $u_n v_n$.

You may want to draw a table to illustrate this. Now, if we add the frequencies for the two possible genotypes, we are going to get

$$\begin{cases} \tilde{u}_{n+1} = u_n^2 + 0.25v_n^2 + u_n v_n \\ \tilde{v}_{n+1} = 0.5v_n^2 + u_n v_n \end{cases}$$

However, the numbers $\tilde{u}_{n+1}, \tilde{v}_{n+1}$ will not add to 1 (that is the subtlety I mentioned) since some of the combinations of the parental alleles are not viable. So to turn them into frequencies, we will have to divide by their sum:

$$\begin{cases} u_{n+1} = \dfrac{u_n^2 + 0.25v_n^2 + u_n v_n}{u_n^2 + 0.75v_n^2 + 2u_n v_n} \\ v_{n+1} = \dfrac{0.5v_n^2 + u_n v_n}{u_n^2 + 0.75v_n^2 + 2u_n v_n} \end{cases}$$

(b) Note that

$$p_n^2 = u_n^2 + 0.25v_n^2 + u_n v_n, \text{ and}$$

$$p_n q_n = p_n(1 - p_n) = p_n - p_n^2 = 0.5v_n u_n + 0.25v_n^2.$$

This gives

$$p_{n+1} = \frac{p_n^2 + p_n q_n}{p_n^2 + 2p_n q_n} = \frac{p_n}{p_n + p_n q_n} = \frac{p_n}{p_n(2 - p_n)}.$$

(c) Suppose $p_n < 1$. Then

$$p_{n+1} - p_n = \frac{p_n}{p_n(2 - p_n)} - p_n = \frac{p_n(1 - 2p_n + p_n^2)}{p_n(2 - p_n)} = \frac{(p_n - 1)^2}{p_n(2 - p_n)} > 0.$$

Thus, the sequence p_n is increasing (unless there was no allele a present in the population to begin with). Let us denote

$$p = \lim_{n \to \infty} p_n.$$

Since

$$\lim_{n \to \infty} p_n = \lim_{n \to \infty} p_{n+1} = \lim_{n \to \infty} \frac{p_n}{p_n(2 - p_n)} = p,$$

we get

$$p = \frac{p}{p(2 - p)},$$

so $p = 1$ or $p = 0$. The latter is not possible, since the aa genotype is not viable (and so $p_1 > 0$). Thus, the limiting frequency of the A allele in the population is 1, and the frequency of the lethal allele a goes to zero over time.

Chapter 3

Problem 1.

(a) Let us denote E the temperature of the environment, which we assume to be constant. Let $T(t)$ (not the best notation, I know) be the temperature of the object as a function of time. Its rate of change is the derivative $T'(t)$. The law states that it is proportional to the difference $(T - E)$, which we can express as

$$T'(t) = h(T(t) - E).$$

Finally, let us determine the sign of the coefficient h. When the object is cooler than the environment (think a frozen pizza in a hot oven), the difference $(T - E)$ is negative, but the rate of change $T'(t)$ is positive (the pizza will warm up). This means that $h < 0$. It may be better to write the law using a positive coefficient $k = -h > 0$, so that it becomes

$$T' = -k(T - E) \text{ or } T' = k(E - T).$$

(b) The equation

$$\frac{dT}{dt} = k(E - T)$$

is separable. Separating the variables gives

$$\int \frac{dT}{E - T} = \int k\,dt + C \text{ or } T = E$$

(I left k on the right-hand side so that dt does not feel lonely). Integration yields

$$-\ln|E - T| = kt + C.$$

Exponentiating both sides, and replacing $\pm e^C$ with a new constant D, gives the general formula

$$E - T = De^{-kt},$$

where $D = E - T_0$ (as usual, $T_0 = T(0)$ stands for the initial temperature). Note that it includes the solution $T = E$, when $D = 0$. So

$$E - T = (E - T_0)e^{-kt}, \text{ or } T = E + (T_0 - E)e^{-kt}.$$

(c) The phase diagram is wonderfully simple, as seen in Figure 42. It expresses the fact that $T(t)$ converges to E monotonely (no surprise here).

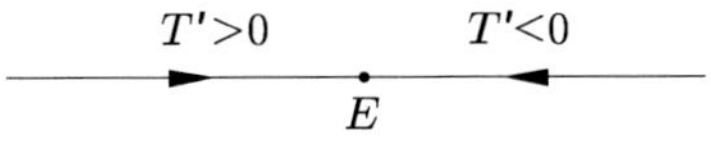

Figure 42. Phase diagram for Newton's law of cooling.

Problem 2.

(a) Let us rewrite the equation as

$$\frac{dy}{dx} = y^2 x.$$

Separation of variables gives

$$\frac{dy}{y^2} = x dx, \text{ or } y \equiv 0.$$

Integrating, we get

$$\int \frac{dy}{y^2} = \int x dx + C,$$

$$-\frac{1}{y} = \frac{x^2}{2} + C,$$

$$y = \frac{2}{D - x^2}, \text{ or } y \equiv 0.$$

(b) Separating the variables and integrating, we get

$$\int e^{2y} dy = \int 3x^2 dx + C,$$

$$\frac{e^{2y}}{2} = x^3 + C,$$

$$y = \frac{1}{2} \ln \left(2x^3 + D \right).$$

(c)

$$\int \frac{dy}{y} = \int \frac{x}{\sqrt{1 + x^2}} dx + C, \text{ or } y \equiv 0.$$

The integration on the right is done using the change of variables $u = 1 + x^2$, so $x dx = \frac{du}{2}$. Carrying it out yields

$$\ln |y| = \sqrt{1 + x^2} + C,$$

$$y = \pm e^C e^{\sqrt{1+x^2}} = D e^{\sqrt{1+x^2}}.$$

Note that this formula includes the solution $y \equiv 0$ (when $D = 0$).

Problem 3. Setting $f(t, x) = x^{1/3}$, we see that

$$\frac{\partial}{\partial x} f(t, x) = \frac{1}{3} x^{-\frac{2}{3}} = \frac{1}{3\sqrt[3]{x^2}},$$

which is not defined when $x = 0$, so the theorem does not apply.

Separating the variables, we get

$$\int x^{-\frac{1}{3}} dx = \int dt + C \text{ or } x \equiv 0.$$

Integration gives

$$\frac{3}{2} x^{\frac{2}{3}} = t + C,$$

so

$$x^2 = \left(\frac{2}{3}(t + C) \right)^3,$$

and $x(0) = 0$ implies that $C = 0$. Applying the square root, we get

$$x = \pm \sqrt{\left(\frac{2}{3} t \right)^3}.$$

We thus get three different formulas, the two given by the above equation, and $x \equiv 0$. Note that the first two formulas are only defined for $t \geq 0$. Thus, there is a unique graph which agrees with the slope field for $t < 0$ (given by $x(t) = 0$), and three different graphs which agree with the slope field for $t \geq 0$.

Problem 4. The equation should have the form

$$x' = f(x),$$

where the function $f(x)$ has zeros at 0, 2, 4, and is positive in the intervals $(-\infty, 0) \cup (2, 4)$ and is negative in $(0, 2) \cup (4, \infty)$. If we take the polynomial

$$p(x) = x(x - 2)(x - 4),$$

it will have the zeros at 0, 2, 4, and will change the sign at these three points. However, to the left of 0 it is negative, which is the opposite of what we need. So we can set $f(x) = -p(x)$, and it will satisfy all of the required properties. The corresponding equation is

$$x' = -x(x - 2)(x - 4).$$

Of course, this is not the only possible answer. We could, for instance, multiply the right-hand side by any positive function, or, say, replace x with x^3 to obtain the same phase diagram.

Problem 5. Note that the assumptions mean that $f(x)$ has no other zeros, except for 0 and 1. Since both of these points are stable, we have $f(x) < 0$ to the right of 0 and $f(x) > 0$ to the left of 1 (drawing a phase diagram could be helpful to visualize this). Of course (by Intermediate Value Theorem) this means that $f(x) = 0$ at some point $x \in (0,1)$, which contradicts our assumptions. Hence, such $f(x)$ does not exist.

Problem 6. We have

$$\frac{dL}{dt} = -r\exp(at)L,$$

so

$$\int \frac{dL}{L} = -\int r\exp(at)dt + B \text{ or } L \equiv 0.$$

Integrating gives

$$\ln|L| = -\frac{r}{a}\exp(at) + B.$$

Exponentiating both sides, we obtain

$$L = \pm\exp(B)\exp\left(-\frac{r}{a}\exp(at)\right).$$

Setting $C = \pm\exp(B)$, we get the desired formula

$$L = C\exp\left(-\frac{r}{a}\exp(at)\right),$$

which also includes the special case $L \equiv 0$ when $D = 0$.

Problem 7. Let us look for the equilibrium solutions:

$$x(M - x) - \frac{ax}{1 + x} = 0.$$

This translates into

$$x[(M - x)(1 + x) - a] = 0.$$

One equilibrium solution is $x = 0$. In brackets, we have a quadratic equation:

$$-x^2 + (M - 1)x + (M - a) = 0.$$

The quadratic formula gives two roots

$$x_{1,2} = \frac{(1 - M) \pm \sqrt{(M - 1)^2 + 4(M - a)}}{-2},$$

however, only one of them is positive (since $M > a$):

$$x_1 = \frac{(M - 1) + \sqrt{(M - 1)^2 + 4(M - a)}}{2} > 0.$$

Draw the phase diagram to check that $x = x_1$ is stable, and $x = 0$ is unstable, so assuming $x(0) \neq 0$, we will have

$$x(t) \xrightarrow[t \to +\infty]{} x_1.$$

Chapter 4

Problem 1.

(a) Suppose

$$c_1 F_1(t) + c_2 F_2(t) \equiv \begin{pmatrix} 0 \\ 0 \end{pmatrix}$$

Looking at the second coordinate, we see that the function

$$g(t) = c_1 t + c_2 t^2 \equiv 0.$$

The derivative

$$g'(t) = c_1 + 2c_2 t \equiv 0,$$

and so $c_1 = g'(0) = 0$. Hence $c_2 = g(1) = 0$ as well.

(b) We only need to prove the "only if" direction. Let us argue by induction on N. For the base of the induction, $N = 0$ and

$$P(t) = c_0 \equiv 0,$$

which implies that $c_0 = 0$.

Now let us assume that the statement holds if the degree of the polynomial is equal to $N - 1$, and let us consider

$$P(t) = c_0 + c_1 t + c_2 t^2 + \cdots + c_N t^N \equiv 0.$$

The derivative

$$P'(t) = c_1 + 2c_2 t + 3c_3 t^2 + \cdots + N c_N t^{N-1}$$

is a polynomial of degree $N - 1$, and $P'(t) \equiv 0$. The induction assumption implies that

$$c_1 = c_2 = \cdots = c_N = 0,$$

hence

$$P(t) = c_0 \equiv 0,$$

which means that $c_0 = 0$ as well.

Problem 2. The system has the form

$$\begin{cases} x' = 1 - xy \\ y' = x^3 - y \end{cases}$$

The Jacobian is

$$\text{Jac}_{x,y} = \begin{pmatrix} -y & -x \\ 3x^2 & -1 \end{pmatrix}$$

As we have already seen, the equilibrium points are $(-1, -1)$ and $(1, 1)$.

$$\text{Jac}_{-1,-1} = \begin{pmatrix} 1 & 1 \\ 3 & -1 \end{pmatrix},$$

its characteristic equation is

$$\lambda^2 - 4 = 0,$$

so the eigenvalues are ± 2. Thus, $(-1, -1)$ is a saddle, which is, of course, and unstable equilibrium.

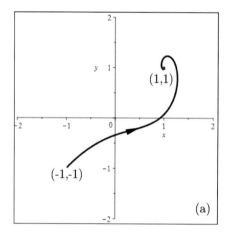
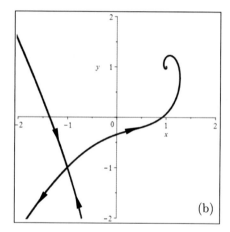
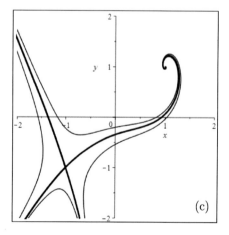

Figure 43. Steps in drawing the phase portrait for Problem 2

The Jacobian

$$\text{Jac}_{1,1} = \begin{pmatrix} -1 & -1 \\ 3 & -1 \end{pmatrix}$$

has eigenvalues $-1 \pm \sqrt{3}i$, so $(1,1)$ is a stable spiral point.

The steps of drawing the phase portrait are illustrated in Figure 43. Saddles are generally our best friends in exercises like this one: their separatrices are an excellent starting point in putting the picture together. Let us begin by connecting the saddle at $(-1,-1)$ with a separatrix to the stable point at $(1,1)$ (Figure 43 (a)). This unstable separatrix has a counterpart on the other side of the saddle, which must go off to infinity. There are two more special trajectories at the saddle point, which are the stable separatrices (arriving from infinity). The picture of separatrices is in Figure 43 (b). The arrows indicate the direction of movement along these curves as t increases. Now, we can add some typical trajectories to the phase portrait, which follow the traffic rules set by the separatrices. The end result is in Figure 43 (c).

Problem 3. The examples are quite similar, so I will only go over the solution of (a). The x-nullcline is given by

$$2x - 2xy = 0,$$

which means that either $x = 0$, or $y = 1$. The x-nullcline thus consists of one vertical and one horizontal lines. The equation for the y-nullcline is the straight line

$$y = 2 - x.$$

The two equilibrium points, which are the intersections of the x- and y-nullclines lie at $(0,2)$ and $(1,1)$. The arrows showing directions of the trajectories are indicated in Figure 44 (left).

The Jacobian is

$$\text{Jac}_{x,y} = \begin{pmatrix} 2 - 2y & -2x \\ -1 & -1 \end{pmatrix}$$

Plugging in $(0,2)$, we get the matrix

$$\text{Jac}_{0,2} = \begin{pmatrix} -2 & 0 \\ -1 & -1 \end{pmatrix}$$

whose eigenvalues are $-1, -2$. This point is a stable node.

The Jacobian at $(1,1)$ has eigenvalues $-1, 2$, so the point is a saddle, which is unstable. On the right of Figure 44 you can see the phase portrait with some typical trajectories. Thicker lines indicate the separatrices of the saddle, which are a good starting point for the picture.

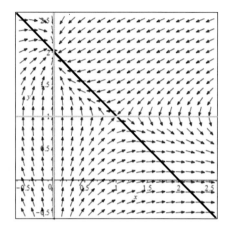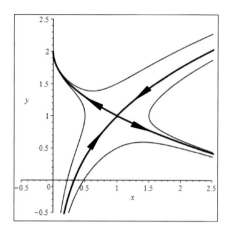

Figure 44. Illustration to Problem 2 (a).

Problem 4. The equilibrium points are $(0,0)$, $(1,0)$, $(0,0.75)$, and $(0.5,0.5)$. The Jacobian of the system is

$$\mathrm{Jac}_{x,y} = \left(\begin{array}{cc} 1 - 2x - y & -x \\ -0.5y & 0.75 - 2y - 0.5x \end{array} \right)$$

To determine the stability of the "coexistence" equilibrium $(0.5, 0.5)$ we could linearize the system at that point. But just for the fun of it, let us linearize at the point $(1,0)$ instead, to see whether it is stable or not. That should be enough to determine the behaviour of the model.

$$\mathrm{Jac}_{1,0} = \left(\begin{array}{cc} -1 & -1 \\ 0 & 0.25 \end{array} \right)$$

The benefit of doing it at $(1,0)$ is that we get an upper-triangular matrix, whose eigenvalues -1, 0.25 are the terms on the diagonal (check this). Hence, the equilibrium $(1,0)$ is a saddle, and thus, $(0,0.75)$ is also a saddle and $(0.5, 0.5)$ is a stable equilibrium point – predicting peaceful coexistence of the two species. A phase portrait showing the separatrices is in Figure 45.

Problem 5.

(a) Setting the right-hand sides equal to zero, we see that either $u = 0$, $v = 0$ or

$$(1 + \alpha u)(1 + \beta v) = u \text{ and } (1 + \alpha u)(1 + \beta v) = v.$$

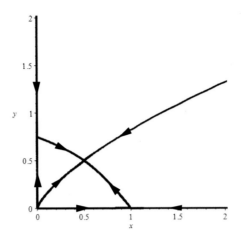

Figure 45. Phase portrait for Problem 3

This, in particular, means that $u = v$ at an equilibrium point. Setting $\alpha = \beta$, we get a quadratic equation

$$(1 + \alpha u)^2 = u.$$

Substituting $\alpha = 0.2$, and using the quadratic formula, we get two more positive equilibrium points, whose coordinates are, approximately,

$$(1.91, 1.91) \text{ and } (13.1, 13.1).$$

Note that when $\alpha = \beta$, there is a symmetry in the Jacobi matrix at each of the equilibrium points, which makes it look like this:

$$\begin{bmatrix} a & b \\ -b & -a \end{bmatrix}$$

for some real a, b. The characteristic equation for such a matrix has the form

$$\lambda^2 = a^2 - b^2,$$

so there are only two possibilities for the linearization: either a saddle ($a^2 > b^2$) or a center ($a^2 < b^2$). Of course, linearization is not going to be of much help in the second case.

I leave it to you to check that $(0,0)$ is a saddle (as it should be in a predator-prey system: prey thrive without predators, predators starve without prey; the stable and unstable separatrices are aligned with the coordinate axes), $(13.1, 13.1)$ is also a saddle, and linearization at

$(1.91, 1.91)$ has a center, which does not tell us what the type/stability of this equilibrium point is.

(b) The phase portrait for the system is shown in Figure 46. It has some very interesting features. The stable and unstable manifolds of the saddle $(13.1, 13.1)$ link up and form a loop. Inside of this loop is the equilibrium point $(1.91, 1.91)$, which apparently remains a center for the non-linear system. The behaviour of the ecosystem after the introduction of the foxes is explained by the figure as follows. If we look at the trajectories starting on the lower right (too many rabbits when not enough foxes are introduced) then we see that with time *both* $u(t)$ and $v(t)$ will grow. The blue trajectory in the figure is an illustration of such a scenario, which is what seems to have actually happened in this ecosystem.

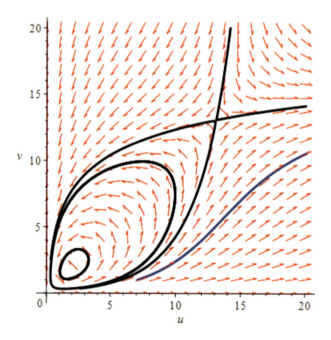

Figure 46. The phase portrait for Problem 5.

Problem 6.

(a) The equilibrium points are $(0, 0)$, $(0, 5)$, $(2, 0)$, $(4, 0)$, $(3, 2)$, and $(3.5, 1.5)$. I will leave the fun of linearizing the system at each one of them to you. The points $(0,0)$, $(4,0)$, $(0,5)$, and $(3,2)$ are saddles, $(2,0)$ is an unstable node, and $(3.5, 1.5)$ is a stable node.

(b) Putting the puzzle together is a fun exercise. I suggest that you start with placing the arrows on the two axes, and then connecting the remaining dots. The result should look as shown in Figure 47. The orcas

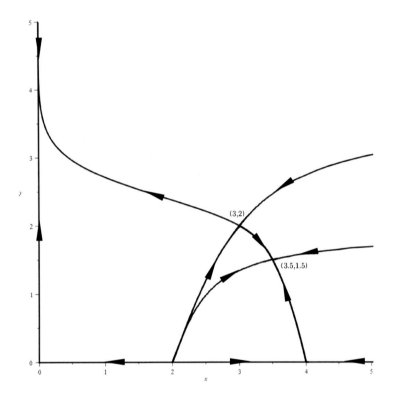

Figure 47. The phase portrait for Problem 6.

survive if the initial conditions are chosen in the region below the stable separatrices of the point $(3,2)$.

Chapter 5

Problem 1.

(a) The phase diagram for $r(t)$ is depicted in Figure 48. Note that r is always non-negative.

Figure 48. The phase diagram for $r(t)$ in Problem 1 (a).

(b) The origin $r = 0$ is an equilibrium point in the above phase diagram, and thus is also an equilibrium point of the two-dimensional phase portrait.

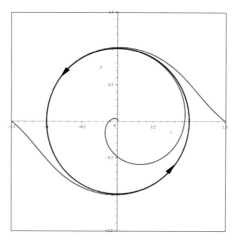

Figure 49. The phase portrait for Problem 1. The limit cycle is shown in black, other trajectories in blue.

From the second equation, the angular coordinate is a linear function of t:

$$\theta(t) = t + \theta_0.$$

The equilibrium point $r = 1$ in the one-dimensional phase diagram becomes a periodic trajectory in two dimension – the unit circle, which is traversed counter-clockwise in time 2π. Since $r = 1$ is attracting in the r direction, the nearby two-dimensional trajectories will spiral towards the unit circle, making it a limit cycle. Clearly, there are no other periodic orbits, or equilibrium points, and the origin is an unstable spiral point.

(c) The two-dimensional phase portrait is shown in Figure 49.

Problem 2. This is fairly easy to do. For instance:

$$\begin{cases} \dfrac{dr}{dt} = r(1-r)(2-r)(3-r) \\[2mm] \dfrac{d\theta}{dt} = 1 \end{cases}$$

Problem 3. Let us take a point inside the limit cycle, and draw a horizontal line segment through it, extending it in both directions until it reaches the cycle (see Figure 50). The horizontal coordinate of a point on the segment will be denoted by x. If we start a trajectory at such a point, it will eventually cross the segment again – let us denote $f(x)$ the position of this crossing, as shown in the figure. The function $f(x)$ is continuous: a small change in the starting point induces a small change in the piece of trajectory. Since the limit cycle attracts nearby trajectories, near the right end of the segment, we have $f(x) > x$ (the point of crossing moves closer to the cycle). Similarly, near the left end, we have $f(x) < x$, so, by Intermediate Value Theorem, there is a point in between at which $f(x) = x$. It obviously is either an equilibrium point or a periodic point, which completes the proof. The function $f(x)$ is known as *Poincaré's first return function*. The

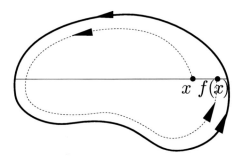

Figure 50. An illustration to Problem 2.

neat idea of using this function to understand trajectories near a limit cycle has been extremely useful in the study of 2D phase portraits. In particular, the proof of Poincaré-Bendixson Theorem is based on it.

Problem 4.

(a) The only equilibrium point satisfying $x \neq 0, y \neq 0$ is $(0.1, 0.54)$. I will leave to you the tedious but straightforward exercise of evaluating the Jacobian at this point and verifying that it is repelling. The two other equilibrium points are $(0,0)$ and $(1,0)$; they are both saddles.

(b) We have
$$\frac{d}{dt}F(x(t), y(t)) = x'(t) + y'(t).$$

Substituting
$$x' = x\left(1 - x - \frac{2y}{1+2x}\right) \text{ and } y' = y\left(-\frac{1}{6} + \frac{2x}{1+2x}\right),$$

and using $y = 6 - x$, gives
$$\frac{d}{dt}F(x,y) = x' + y' = \frac{7}{6}x - x^2 - 1.$$

Let us denote this expression $g(x)$. The function $g(x)$ is quadratic. It is an easy Calculus exercise to see that it has its global maximum at $x_* = \frac{7}{12}$, and $g(x_*) < 0$. Thus, $g(x)$ is negative, which proves that
$$\frac{d}{dt}F(x(t), y(t)) < 0 \text{ on the line } x + y = 6.$$

(c) The x- and y-axes are clearly invariant in this problem (the axes correspond to the absence of one of the species from the ecosystem). In combination with part (b), this means that the triangle T bounded by the two coordinate axes and the line $y = 6 - x$ is forward invariant (see Figure 51, left). This triangle contains the fixed point $(0.1, 0.54)$ inside. Since this point is repelling, for a small enough disk D centered at it, all trajectories through its boundary point *outwards*. Consider the forward invariant region $T \setminus D$ (the triangle with a small disk removed). It does not quite fit the definition of a trapping region, as it has two equilibrium points on the boundary. However, both of them are saddles, whose stable separatrices follow the coordinate axes, and thus, no trajectory which starts in the interior of $T \setminus D$ can converge to either of these points. Poincaré-Bendixson Theorem implies that every trajectory in the interior of the triangle $T \setminus D$ converges to a limit cycle. In fact, there is a single such limit cycle, as shown in Figure 51 (right).

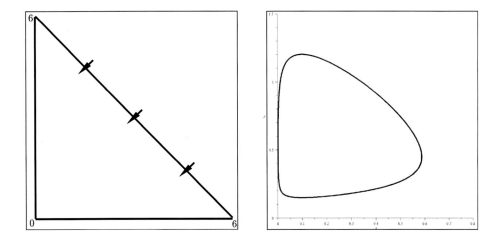

Figure 51. Left: the forward invariant triangle for Problem 5. Right: the limit cycle.

Chapter 6

Problem 1. The infected population $I(t)$ will now be divided into two groups: the treated one, of size $\eta I(t)$, recovering at a rate γ_t, and the untreated one, of size $(1 - \eta)I(t)$, which recovers at a slower rate γ_u. Putting this together, and setting $\delta = 0$, we obtain a modified system given by

$$\begin{cases} S' = -\beta \frac{IS}{N} \\ I' = \beta \frac{IS}{N} - I(\eta\gamma_t + (1-\eta)\gamma_u) \end{cases}$$

If no one gets treated, then $\eta = 0$ and

$$R_0 = \frac{\beta}{\gamma_u}.$$

Otherwise,

$$R_0 = \frac{\beta}{\eta\gamma_t + (1-\eta)\gamma_u} < \frac{\beta}{\gamma_u}.$$

Problem 2. Let $\mu \in (0,1)$ be the probability of an infected mother passing the infection to her daughter. Children in the "Susceptible" and "Recovered" bins are born susceptible, giving a contribution of

$$\delta(S + R) = \delta(N - I)$$

to S'. Infected mothers give birth to non-infected daughters with probability $(1 - \mu)$, giving a further contribution of $\delta(1 - \mu)I$ to S'. On the other hand, $\delta\mu I$ becomes an additional contribution to I', which accounts for the vertical transmission. Putting this together, we get the following system:

$$\begin{cases} S' = \delta(N - S - \mu I) - \beta \frac{IS}{N} \\ I' = -(\delta(1-\mu) + \gamma)I + \beta \frac{IS}{N} \end{cases}$$

Problem 4.

(a) To write the equations of the system, let us divide the population into six compartments rather than three: the first group (with few social connections) will correspond to the compartments S_1, I_1, R_1, and the second group (the "superspreaders") will correspond to S_2, I_2, R_2. Since the first group mixes at a rate ten times less than the second group, the equations of the model will look like this:

$$\begin{cases} S_1' = -\dfrac{\beta}{N}0.1^2 S_1 I_1 - \dfrac{\beta}{N}0.1 S_1 I_2 \\[2mm] S_2' = -\dfrac{\beta}{N}0.1 S_2 I_1 - \dfrac{\beta}{N}S_2 I_2 \\[2mm] I_1' = -\gamma I_1 + \dfrac{\beta}{N}0.1^2 S_1 I_1 + \dfrac{\beta}{N}0.1 S_1 I_2 \\[2mm] I_2' = -\gamma I_2 + \dfrac{\beta}{N}0.1 S_2 I_1 + \dfrac{\beta}{N}S_2 I_2 \end{cases}$$

(b) The results of the numerical simulation of the above system with the initial data $S_1(0) = 810$, $S_2(0) = 90$, $I_1(0) = 90$, $I_2(0) = 10$ (so that 90%/10% ratio holds both for the susceptible and infected groups) is seen in Figure 52. The susceptible population stabilizes at 512, this is the size of the group that avoids being infected.

Figure 52. The results of the simulation for Problem 4. Left – the total susceptible population $S(t) = S_1(t) + S_2(t)$, right – the total infected population $I(t) = I_1(t) + I_2(t)$.

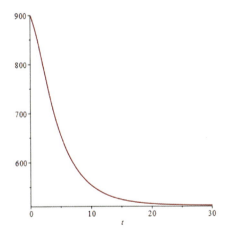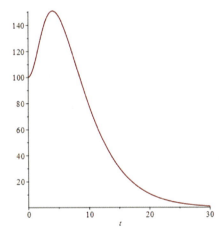

Attributions for the images

- Front cover Ascii art. Original image "Shrewd look" Umair, Flickr commons.
  Converted using a free online Ascii text-art image conversion tool from *https://manytools.org/*

- Figure 1, left. Boeing B777 of British Airways Flickr commons, *https://www.flickr.com/photos/elsie/*

- Figure 3, reptile body parts. Flickr commons, Siyavula Education. Modification: changed captions.

- Figure 5, left. Hand X-ray. Flickr commons, *https://www.flickr.com/photos/therahim/*. Modification: minor deletion.

- Figure 9. From *Wikimedia commons* Public domain. Source: "The physical basis of heredity" by Thomas Hunt Morgan. Philadelphia: J.B. Lippincott Company 1919.

- Problem 5, Chapter 4. Rabbit. Flickr commons, *https://www.flickr.com/photos/lakeworth/*. Modification: flipped horizontally.

- Problem 5, Chapter 4. Calm and attentive fox. Flickr commons, *https://www.flickr.com/photos/tambako/*

Manufactured by Amazon.ca
Bolton, ON